RENTAL PROPERTY AND TAXATION

4th EDITION

AN AUSTRALIAN INVESTOR'S GUIDE

TONY COMPTON

Wrightbooks

Fourth edition first published 2008 by Wrightbooks,
an imprint of John Wiley & Sons Australia, Ltd
42 McDougall Street, Milton Qld 4064

Office also in Melbourne

Typeset in Baskerville 10/14pt

National Library of Australia Cataloguing-in-Publication Data:

Compton, Tony, 1951-
Rental property and taxation : an Australian investor's guide / Tony Compton.
4th ed.

9780731408481 (pbk.)

Includes index.

Real estate investment--Australia. Real estate investment--Taxation--Australia.
Real estate investment--Australia--Finance.

332.63240994

Acknowledgement: The author and publisher would like to thank the Commonwealth
of Australia for kind permission to reproduce extracts from the *Income Tax Assessment
Act 1936* and the *Income Tax Assessment Act 1997*.

All legislative material herein is reproduced by permission but does not purport to be
the official or authorised version. It is subject to Commonwealth of Australia copyright.
The *Copyright Act 1968* permits certain reproduction and publication of Commonwealth
legislation. In particular, s.182A of the Act enables a complete copy to be made by or on
behalf of a particular person. For reproduction or publication beyond that permitted
by the Act, permission should be sought in writing. Requests should be addressed to the
Manager, Copyright Services, Info Access, Department of Finance and Administration,
GPO Box 1920, Canberra City, ACT 2601, or emailed to <Cwealthcopyright@finance.
gov.au>.

Nick Renton / © Nick Renton. Reproduced with permission.

Cover design by Rob Cowpe

Printed in Australia by McPherson's Printing Group

10 9 8 7 6 5 4 3 2 1

Disclaimer: The material in this publication is of the nature of general comment only,
and neither purports nor intends to be advice. Readers should not act on the basis
of any matter in this publication without considering (and if appropriate, taking)
professional advice with due regard to their own particular circumstances. The author
and publisher expressly disclaim all and any liability to any person, whether a purchaser
of this publication or not, in respect of anything and of the consequences of anything
done or omitted to be done by any such person in reliance, whether whole or partial,
upon the whole or any part of the contents of this publication.

Contents

Contents

Preface

There have been many changes since the first edition of this book was written. The number of taxpayers owning rental properties has increased so much so that, according to Australian Tax Office (ATO) statistics, in 2004–05 1 495 645 tax returns were lodged that included gross rent as income. The boom in real estate has meant that capital gains tax has become a very real issue for those who decide to sell their properties. Many couples have paid the price of their short-term decision to invest in the higher income earning partner's name.

Some things, however, remain the same. Real estate property companies continue to hawk rental properties in the various media. People continue to be invited to wealth-creation seminars where they learn how to become financially independent in a relatively short period of time. Telephone canvassers continue to phone at inopportune moments. Pamphlets arrive with other junk mail encouraging negative or positive gearing strategies. Figures are produced that may or may not stand the test of time. Misinformation abounds. For instance, one real estate company's internet site tells its readers 'once you have an investment property you will need to register for an Australian business number. If you want to claim input tax credits on the expenses you incur in running the investment, you will have to register for the GST as well'. They are wrong on both counts.

People continue to make decisions that are tax-driven rather than investment-driven. In my experience, the majority of investors still do not understand the tax implications of their property investment. Many fail to appreciate that it is not enough for them to rely on their accountant to attend to their tax affairs. He or she can only work with the information provided and his or her understanding of the client's affairs. In a self-assessment environment it is important that taxpayers attempt to obtain some understanding of the tax laws as they apply to their own situations. This is a difficult task as Australia's tax legislation is involved, complex and unwieldy, and nothing has happened that suggests to me that this will change. Nevertheless, property investors should make an attempt to be better informed about tax law as it relates to their investment/s.

Despite the government's promises of simplification, tax law continues to become even more complex. Different rules apply for depreciable assets purchased pre–21 September 1999, between 21 September 1999 and before 1 January 2001, and after 1 January 2001. As well as this, pooling provisions have been introduced. Instead of presenting depreciation tables with percentage rates based on the effective lives, the Australian Taxation Office (ATO) has provided effective life tables requiring calculations based on the effective life and advisor of 100 or 200 depending on whether the depreciation method used is prime cost or diminishing value. The ATO instructs that the formula for calculating depreciation on an asset using the diminishing value method is:

Opening undeducted cost × (days owned ÷ 365)
× 200 per cent of the effective life in years

What should be a simple matter has become more difficult, increasing the scope for error. Numerous changes, such as these, have been made since this book was first written. The changes are included in this new edition. Hopefully it will help non-accountants and non-lawyers obtain an understanding of the Australian taxation system as it relates to rental properties.

Tony Compton
Springwood, Qld
March 2008

Disclaimer

It is important that advice be sought from a competent taxation professional before acting on any information provided in this book. Tax laws change, and while every effort has been made to ensure the accuracy of the information herein at the time of writing, it is provided as a general guide only.

Chapter 1

The purchase

Ian and Marie are long-time clients of mine. They operate an earthmoving business, and up until now have lived year to year on an income from which they have saved little. One night, Ian received a phone call from a canvasser selling negatively geared investment properties. He and Marie had paid off their house (with the assistance of a small lottery win) and were interested in the idea of investing, so he agreed to meet with the caller.

As it turned out, the promoter was selling residential units in Chermside (a suburb on Brisbane's northside). Chermside is well serviced by transport, schools and shops, and is reasonably close to the city. He appeared genuine and the couple's interest intensified.

That night, Ian and Marie made the decision to commence a journey into the investment world. Specifically, they decided to look into income-producing residential property.

I heard about it when they came in with their taxation records. They asked my advice, showed me the papers that they received from the investment company and told me they had signed a contract that was subject to finance. My clients knew little about investing, let alone investing in property. Further, they knew nothing about the effect of income tax on the investment. Nevertheless, they decided that they needed to provide for their retirement, and were disillusioned with the poor returns they had been achieving from their superannuation fund.

Income-producing residential property

Despite the lack of capital growth in recent years, I have long been a fan of income-producing residential property—on a long-term basis, that is. Real estate is an illiquid asset. As many have found, it can be hard to sell—particularly at a realistic price—if you need the money quickly. Gains are inconsistent. Prices may stagnate for years, then show a rapid appreciation in a short period of time before going into hibernation again. Despite this, property has a part in everyone's investment portfolio, along with shares, managed trusts and cash funds.

Ian and Marie listened intently as I explained the wisdom of a balanced investment portfolio that comprised assets from the various investment categories. But they, like many, did not have a lot of cash to invest and were borrowing to fund the purchase. They had been advised to negatively gear their purchase and, comfortable with that idea, they had decided to proceed.

Too many people base their decisions on tax savings rather than wealth creation. I have never understood why people would spend a dollar to save, at best, 46.5¢. If that spending does not provide a benefit other than reducing tax, why spend? In many instances the tax saving would only be 16.5¢, which means that a dollar has been spent to save 16.5¢. Some people spend a dollar that they otherwise would not, to save 16.5¢ in tax. Surely they would be better off keeping the dollar. I have lost count of the number of times I have heard that someone has advised the purchase of a new car to help reduce a tax problem. I can't understand why—spending to minimise tax just does not make sense.

My clients understood this; their decision was not tax-driven. They were interested in acquiring an asset to supplement their income upon retirement.

Negative gearing

Marie and Ian asked me to explain negative gearing to them. I told them that it is a simple concept where an investment returns a loss after interest is paid. Gearing relates to the amount of borrowing in an investment. Today, many rental properties are 100 per cent geared. None of the owners' cash is tied up. They are funded by making up for any valuation shortfall by giving a mortgage over the owners' residence.

In an economy where property values are rising, negative gearing results in incredibly high returns. Suppose a property is purchased for $110000 using only $10000 of the owners' capital. If the property's value increases to $120000 in one year, a 100 per cent return of the investment has been achieved. Leverage is obtained by using someone else's money to make money for yourself. However, the higher the gearing the higher the risk and, as some have found, the higher the loss.

In whose name?

Ian and Marie had a joint taxable income of $80000. Divided equally, this resulted in tax payable of $9500 each (at 2007–08 income tax rates). Their marginal tax rate was 31.5 per cent including the Medicare levy. This means that for every extra dollar they earned they paid 31.5¢ in tax.

The contract they had signed was in joint names. I explained to them that property income is distributed in accordance with the ownership. That means that any profit or loss from the rental property would be shared equally.

They told me that a friend had told them that the property should be purchased by Ian. 'Friends' cause a lot of trouble in this profession. Seldom is the advice they have so generously given correct. I have lost count of the hours wasted explaining that you can't claim for the raffle tickets purchased in the local art union; or you can't claim for driving your car to and from work every day; or that you can't claim for the cost of renovating a run-down property so that you can rent it out.

Seldom does the case arise where I can agree that a rental property should be purchased in one spouse's name only—even if one of the partners is not working. For me, property investment is long term: I believe in buying and holding forever so that one day the property will become income-positive. While in the first years there is the advantage of being able to offset a loss against the income of higher earning husband or wife, there is also the disadvantage of the loss eventually turning to profit and adding to his or her taxable income. Further, if a property is sold and a capital gain is made, that gain would be incurred solely by the person on the higher income. This course of action does not make sense. No-one has been able to give me a satisfactory solution to this problem. Some suggestions include, 'Buy another property', but this would compound the problem. 'Sell half the property to the spouse, then.' What about the capital gain, legal fees and stamp duty payable? I remain to be convinced.

There has only been one clear instance in my years of practice when a property should have been, and was, purchased by the breadwinner. The client, who is a doctor and friend, was earning over $150 000 per year. He wanted to buy a block of units and the tax savings far outweighed any later disadvantage, particularly given that he and his wife already owned other properties.

This issue wasn't a problem for Ian and Marie. They had decided themselves that joint ownership was for the better.

I have read an opinion that if property is bought short term with no borrowings, then ownership should be with the lowest income earner. Furthermore, if it is purchased long term with maximum borrowing it should be in the name of the highest income earner.

A calculation was provided showing the effect of the holding over five and ten years to support the argument.

If only it was that easy. In the first instance, property is a long-term investment, not short term, and even ten years is not long term in this context. Further, the assumption is made that the property will be negatively geared for the period of the ownership. I don't believe that is appropriate in a non-inflationary environment. The result would have been different if the calculations had been made over a longer period of time, and based on a principal and interest loan.

Interest-only loans

The unit salesperson had suggested Marie and Ian take out an interest-only loan to finance their investment. Again, I shook my head. This may be sound advice in a period of rapid inflation when property values are increasing, but not in an economy where inflation is low, such as in the 1990s and early to mid 2000s. Why rent a loss? This is what you are doing with interest-only money when values are showing little or no growth. The only time interest-only money should be used in a non-inflationary climate is when there are other loans on non–income-producing assets, such as your residence. In this case you are better off getting an interest-only loan for the rental property and using any surplus funds to repay the non–tax-deductible loan off as quickly as possible. Once that is achieved, you should convert to a principal and interest loan.

You need to look at why you are investing. At some time you will want to be debt-free. Most of us will not want to be burdened with debt when we retire, so an appropriate strategy should be in place to prevent this—and an interest-only loan in a deflationary economy does not fit this description.

An opinion has been expressed that principal and interest loans have a disadvantage because, as the amount of interest decreases with the principal repayment, a loss of tax benefits results with the reduction in allowable deductions. You can't be worse off by earning an extra dollar. You can be by spending one. By reducing your interest debt you are increasing the net return from your rental property. The goal should be to reduce the costs, not increase them.

Interest-only loans are normally for a short fixed period. Every first-year accounting student is taught that borrowing short to finance long is to court financial disaster. Losses can occur when, at the time of refinancing, the lender is not prepared to carry on with the loan, and the property has to be sold in haste.

Construction cost write-off

The property at Chermside was six years old. This was an advantage in that a non-cash tax deduction exists for residential income properties on which construction commenced after

18 July 1985. People who purchase properties that were commenced between 18 July 1985 and 15 September 1987 are eligible for a 4 per cent allowance on the cost of construction. There is a 2.5 per cent discount for those who purchase properties commenced after this date. A 2.5 per cent annual claim is available for structural improvements commenced after 27 February 1992.

Once again, the purchase decision should not be made on the basis of the availability of this benefit. A property in a good area that shows consistent growth over a period of time may provide better gains than a property that qualifies for the write-off, but that is situated in a less affluent or profitable location.

Using a real estate agent

The person selling the property to Ian and Marie was not a real estate agent. He was a property marketer who sold negative-gearing schemes. As part of the lure to buy from him, he offered a guaranteed rental for two years. Ian is street-wise and passed that up. You can be sure that any guaranteed rentals will be above the market and will be paid for by the purchaser in the purchase price. He negotiated a lower price and decided to use an agent to find a tenant. The area in which my clients had purchased lets easily, but he felt the commissions an agent charges more than compensates for the hassles of finding a tenant, attending to minor maintenance problems and collecting the rent. My view regarding the engagement of real estate agents as property managers has done a complete shift from the view I had when I wrote earlier editions of this book. I have heard too many tales of poor management practice from clients, convincing me that it is something that should be done with great care, if at all.

Key points

- Income-producing residential properties have a place in every investment portfolio, along with shares, managed trusts and cash.

- The purchase should be investment-driven rather than tax-driven.

- Property is a long-term investment. With this in mind, seek advice from a tax professional as to how the ownership should be constructed.

- Give careful thought to your circumstances before accepting that an interest-only loan is right for you.

- A property in a good location without non-cash deductions may provide a better long-term gain than one with non-cash deductions in a less affluent or profitable location.

- The advantages of using a real estate agent to manage the property should outweigh the costs.

Chapter 2

The tax return

A year passed and Ian and Marie returned to my office with their annual income tax information, which for the first time included their rental property records. They opened the concertina file in which they had stored their records and proceeded to give me the details required.

The settlement statement

The first document they produced was the statement sent to them by their solicitor when the property was settled. I recorded the details, and placed them in a file marked 'Capital gains information'. This would need to be kept for five years after the property was sold or, if a loss was incurred, until five years after it could be offset against an assessable capital gain.

The information I recorded included:

- the date of acquisition
- the cost of the property
- other costs of purchasing, including solicitor's fees, search fees and stamp duty.

The loan documents

They then handed me the loan documentation. I recorded the borrowing expenses, which are the costs of arranging finance for the rental property. These should be treated carefully: if they total less than $100 they can be claimed in the year of payment; if they exceed $100 they must be written off over the shorter of either the period of the loan or five years.

Loan application fees, legal costs in relation to the mortgage, stamp duty on the loan, fees for the registration of documents, title searches, mortgage registration, valuations and mortgage insurance premiums all form part of borrowing costs.

Ian and Marie said they had a friend who had been unsuccessful with a loan application. Finance was later obtained elsewhere. They asked if their friend could claim the costs of both loans. After telling them their friend should obtain the advice professionally, I explained to them that you can only claim the costs for loans that are proceeded with. In other words, if you apply for a loan and are knocked back, you cannot claim the costs associated with the unsuccessful application.

Income

It was then time to record the income. Income tax is payable on the taxable income you earn in a financial year. In Australia, the financial year runs from 1 July to 30 June. Your taxable income is the assessable income you earn less the allowable deductions you incur in that period.

Assessable income is made up of ordinary income and other amounts (such as capital gains) that are specifically included in assessable income.

The rent that you receive is assessable income. That is, the gross rent—which is what you receive before anything is deducted—is the amount that you must declare as rental income, not the amount received after deductions.

Other amounts received (such as bond reimbursements for repairs, cleaning or rent arrears) also form part of your assessable income.

There are two methods of returning income for tax purposes:

1   The *cash basis*, which recognises income when it is received.

2   The *accrual method*, which recognises income when it is earned.

Rental income is declared under the cash basis. This means that you include your rental income in the year in which you receive it. If an agent receives the money for you, you declare the income in the year the tenant pays him or her, not the year in which you receive the cheque. This is because the agent is acting on your behalf, and it is deemed that you have received the rent when he or she has received it.

Ian and Marie nodded in understanding, but I often wonder just how much of our complex tax system many clients actually comprehend.

Agent's rental statements

They handed me the monthly rental statements that had been sent to them by the agent managing the property, and also produced an annual summary. I ignored the annual statement and proceeded to enter the monthly figures into a spreadsheet, reconciling the net amount paid to the deposits on my clients' rental property bank statements. Too many times I have encountered agents' statements that do not correspond to the annual statements. Figures have sometimes been omitted or expenses have been aggregated. Sometimes this has been the result of a change in the agent's software. The onus is on the taxpayer to ensure the information is correct. For that reason, I strongly advise people to check the details on their annual rental statements. Hopefully, their experience will be different to that of many clients of mine

Expenditure

My clients asked what else could be deducted. I told them to hold on, I was working through that and would explain as I went on. I started by telling them that care must be taken to claim only those deductions which are allowable. Not all costs incurred are deductible. You need to differentiate between those costs that are defined as capital and those that are an expense.

For an expense to be an allowable deduction, the property must be rented or available for rent. The initial costs of preparing a property for rental are not deductible. The couple had been told that if they painted the unit before it was rented they could make a claim. This is incorrect—there is a difference between maintenance and improvement. I told Marie and Ian that, rather than jumping ahead and causing confusion, I would discuss this later when we came to the claim for repairs and maintenance (see chapter 14).

Apportionment for part-year use

Ian had a job in New South Wales for three weeks. While he was away, Marie's mother took ill and was admitted to a hospital near the unit. The tenant had vacated and the new tenant was not due to take up residency for two weeks, so Marie moved in to be close to the hospital. This necessitated an adjustment to the expenses claimed. The property had been owned for 11 months of the financial year, so I explained that I would need to show 4.5 per cent of the expenses, excluding the agent's management fees, as being of a private nature. While not very happy about this, my clients understood that they had to comply with the tax laws, and the adjustment was made.

An adjustment for apportioning private use is often made by the tax office when auditing rental returns. This is more commonly appropriate to holiday rentals where the owners stay for a period of time during the year.

I like to keep things in order, so I said we would proceed through the remainder of the claims in alphabetic progression.

Advertising

The property Ian and Marie purchased was vacant. The agent advertised and found a tenant, and the cost of the advertisement was shown on the rental statements provided by the agent.

I explained that the costs of advertising a property to obtain a tenant are a deduction. The costs of advertising your property for sale are not, but will be a cost for capital gains tax (CGT) purposes.

So, if you pay your agent to place an ad in the newspaper to find a tenant (or you do it yourself) you can claim the costs as an allowable deduction.

Agent's commission and charges

Because Ian and Marie paid an agent to manage the property for them, the costs are deductible. This includes the agent's commission, letting fees and sundry charges. These details were shown on the monthly statements the agent sent them.

Bank charges

My clients had followed the advice I had given them when we first discussed the rental property, opening a bank account solely for transactions relating to the property.

They knew that they could claim the charges for operating a bank account used for banking rent and paying rental expenses. They also realised that if the account was used for other purposes, an apportionment would need to be made for private use. I like to keep things simple. My clients felt the same, so they opened a separate account. I extracted the charges and periodic loan costs (such as loan service fees), which are also deductible, from their bank statements.

Body corporate fees

The property Ian and Marie purchased was strata-titled, and incurred body corporate fees. These costs are deductible, and they handed me the statements from the body corporate manager so that these could be claimed.

Borrowing costs

I looked at the information I had extracted from the loan documentation and apportioned the borrowing costs. The loan was over 20 years, so the costs were divided by 1825 (5 years x 365 days—refer to 'The loan documents' on page 10) and multiplied by 334 (the days between the incurring of the costs and the end of the financial year) to apportion the year's claim. A note was prepared detailing the annual claim for the next five years and attached to the front of the file for easy access.

Cleaning

After the first tenant vacated, it was necessary to have the property cleaned. My clients' agent arranged for this to happen and a claim was made on the basis of the costs disclosed on the rental statement. If Ian and Marie had cleaned the unit themselves they could have claimed the costs of materials; however, no claim could be made for their time. The only cost for your time is an opportunity cost—the cost of forgoing another activity. There is no monetary cost.

Computer costs

Ian and Marie had been in business for many years, but for various reasons they had resisted using a computer. However, with the purchase of the property, they decided it was time to make the plunge and adopt the technology.

If you use a computer to maintain your property records, you can claim the costs incurred. These include depreciation, software and stationery. However, you must apportion the private usage. To do this you should keep a log of the time the computer is used for both rental and private use, and make your claim accordingly. Generally, a one-month record will suffice. Software purchased solely for maintenance of property records should be claimed in total as it is unlikely that it would be used for anything other than rental property reckoning.

Capital allowances (decline in value)

Being in business, Ian and Marie knew that certain items that would not otherwise be claimable could be depreciated and claimed against their rental income.

Depreciation has been replaced by the tax term 'decline in value'. This is a special deduction that allows you to write off a proportion of the cost of plant used to produce assessable income in that financial year. There are two methods for calculating the decline in value for tax purposes:

1   The *prime cost* method—which calculates depreciation as a percentage of the cost of the plant.

2   The *diminishing value* method—which is based on the cost of the asset in the first year, and then as a percentage of the depreciated cost for following years.

I prefer to use the diminishing value basis, as it gives a higher claim in the earlier years. This takes advantage of the fact that, in inflationary times, a dollar today is worth more than a dollar tomorrow.

You must own the item of plant to claim this deduction and you cannot claim for the cost of furniture owned by the tenant. My clients had decided to furnish the unit and the furniture was depreciated accordingly.

Because the plant was owned for only part of the financial year, the amount calculated needed to be apportioned over the period of ownership. For example, the refrigerator they purchased and installed in the rental property on 1 April was claimed for the period 1 April to 30 June only. This is calculated by multiplying the cost by the appropriate rate, in this case 16.66 per cent (200 ÷ 12 years—see chapter 7), dividing by 365 (the days in the year) and multiplying by 91 (the days the appliance was installed and ready for use).

In most instances the pooling provisions of the tax legislation should be used for assets costing less than $1000 and more than $300. These items can be written off at 18.75 per cent in the first year and 37.5 per cent in following years. No prorating of the rate is necessary in the first year.

Items of plant costing less than $301 can be claimed in the year the asset is installed ready for use. This write-off is not available if the total cost of it and other identical or substantially identical items purchased in the same year exceeds $300.

As is normal, the cost of carpets, stoves, hot-water systems and other items available for this claim were not apportioned when my clients purchased their rental property. At the original meeting they had asked how to ascertain the cost of these. I had said that, in my opinion, the benefits of having a quantity surveyor prepare a depreciation report far exceed the costs. Often, items such as common property in a strata title environment will be overlooked if you attempt to apportion the costs yourself. And it would be extremely difficult for the tax office to challenge values based on a report prepared by an independent surveyor. Ian and Marie had taken my advice and handed over the report they had had prepared.

If they had chosen to apportion values themselves, they would have needed to ensure that the values were reasonable (just in case they were asked to justify the values at some time in the future). If they had apportioned values themselves, they should have used relevant market values at the time of the making of the contract. This does not mean the cost of replacing the asset, but rather what it is worth at that time. This should have taken into account notional depreciation incurred from the date of the original purchase.

Gardening and grounds maintenance

The costs of maintaining the grounds of the property, such as lawn mowing, rubbish removal and tree lopping, may be claimed as an allowable deduction. Ian and Marie did not incur a cost for these, as they were the responsibility of the body corporate.

Insurance

I asked for the insurance invoices and was given documentation for landlords' insurance, public indemnity insurance and the cost of insuring the property, which were all deductible.

Interest

The loan statements provided the requisite details of interest paid during the year.

I had previously explained that interest incurred on borrowings used to produce assessable income is deductible. It is the purpose of the borrowing that is important, not the asset against which the loan is secured. If you own your home and use it as collateral for the purchase of a rental property, you can claim the interest. You cannot claim the interest on a loan to finance the house in which you live. That is, if you own a rental property and borrow against it to finance your residence, there can be no claim.

I had no intention of entering into a discussion about split loans with my clients. Their friend had one and I advised that any questions he had as to the deductibility of the interest on those loans should be directed to his professional adviser. (Chapter 11 discusses split loans.)

Land tax

Ian and Marie didn't own sufficient property to be liable for land tax. If they had been unlucky enough to have a land tax liability, some comfort could have been taken in that the payment of the liability is an allowable deduction.

Legal fees

Legal fees for drawing up a lease, issuing demands on a tenant and attending to the discharge of a loan can be claimed. Legal fees on the purchase or sale of a property are of a capital nature and cannot be claimed as a deduction.

Letting fees

After a tenant vacated and a new tenant needed to be found, my clients' agent charged a letting fee equivalent to one week's rent to find a new tenant. This fee was claimed as a deduction against the rental income received, and was disclosed on the agent's rental statements. Care should be taken to ensure that the agent has not netted off the cost. You are required to declare all assessable income and should claim all allowable deductions. Although a set-off would result in the same net effect, a return prepared on this basis would understate both income and deductions.

Management fees

The property Ian and Marie's friend owned, as is common with holiday units, was managed. The manager arranges rentals, pays common costs and charges a commission for the work done. These costs are much the same as an agent's commission, and are deductible against the rental earned. I wondered that their friend should pay for the time I was taking to answer their questions on his behalf. I was wanting to concentrate on the job at hand and feeling uncomfortable about the advice being given for a non-client. Still, Ian and Marie were clients of long standing, so I kept my thoughts to myself.

Mortgage discharge

If my clients were able to pay out the loan on their rental property, the costs of discharging the mortgage would be deductible. This includes their solicitor's costs and any charges levied by their lender.

Motor running

The substantiation rules (under which claims for work-related expenses, car expenses and travelling expenses must be substantiated to be allowed) apply to motor running. It is unlikely that a landlord would travel more than 5000 kilometres a year in attending to the needs of his or her properties. Therefore, in most cases the set rate per kilometre basis would be the appropriate basis for a claim against rental income.

This method allows a claim of the rental–expense-related mileage based on a reasonable estimate of the kilometres travelled and the engine size of your vehicle. You cannot just make a guess at the mileage. It is in your best interest to record the actual kilometres travelled so that there can be no dispute as to the basis of your estimate. The maximum claim under this method is 5000 kilometres. Table 2.1 shows the motor running rates as at 2008–09.

Table 2.1: motor running rates

Engine capacity rate non-rotary engine	Rate per km
up to 1600cc	58¢
1600cc to 2600cc	69¢
over 2600cc	70¢

I explained to Ian and Marie that rent expense mileage includes travel to collect rent, inspect the property, attend to repairs, bank rental income, an accountant for tax advice and to attend to other matters in respect of their income-producing property. As their agent collected the rent, they had no claim for motor running for rent collection.

They asked about motor vehicle expenses in inspecting the property prior to purchase or attending to improvements before the property was rented. I advised that these were not deductible.

From their business experience, they knew that if they travelled more than 5000 kilometres they would need to calculate the method which gave them the biggest deduction, selecting from:

- the set rate method
- 12 per cent of cost
- one-third of running expenses
- actual costs.

Repairs and maintenance

As their property was a recent acquisition, Ian and Marie had not incurred many expenses for repairs. There was a cost for an electrician to replace an element on the stove but, apart from repairs to the hot-water system, that was the only work that had been done. I explained that the replacement of the hot-water system was a non-deductible capital expense but that it could be depreciated.

The area least understood by clients in respect of rental properties would have to be the distinction between repairs of a claimable nature and improvements. Repairs are costs incurred in restoring an asset to the condition it was in at the time the asset was first used by its owner to earn income. An improvement takes the asset beyond that condition. When repairs and improvements are made at the same time, landlords should ensure that the relevant costs are segregated.

Income tax returns, which include rental income, are commonly adjusted on audit because initial capital improvements have been claimed as repairs.

Safe deposit boxes

Aware of the need to keep their records in a safe place, Ian and Marie hired a safe deposit box at the bank. Record keeping was the sole reason for the box, and a claim was made accordingly.

Secretarial and bookkeeping expenses

Marie kept the records of her friend's rental property, diligently recording the income as it was received and the expenses as they were paid. He paid her a fee for this. This became assessable income to Marie, and was claimable by her friend.

Care must be taken to ensure that such payments are commercially realistic. Some property marketers advise clients who have purchased a property in their own name to pay their spouse a bookkeeping fee. The work must be carried out and the payment made in order to make a claim. The spouse must then declare the income in his or her return.

I wonder sometimes at the ethics behind advice that recommends paying these fees, particularly when the property is in the hands of an agent, or the owner does the work and the spouse does nothing. It isn't worth acting outside the taxation laws. Why take such risks when the penalties can be so great? If you pay bookkeeping fees to a spouse, make sure that the amount paid is what you would pay an unrelated person for doing the work.

Tax advice costs

Next I made a claim for the fee I charged Ian and Marie for advice on the taxation implications of their purchase.

Telephone

My clients kept a record of telephone calls made to the agent, tradespeople and other business relating to the investment property. There were relatively few of these and they were claimed on the basis of the number of calls made at the rate applicable per call.

Travel

In my clients' case, their travel claim was limited to their motor running. However, travel costs incurred to inspect and supervise income-producing properties are claimable. Common sense must prevail here. If you own a rental property interstate and have a holiday there, you would find it difficult to convince a tax auditor that the travel costs relate to the inspection of the property.

Ian and Marie gathered up their documents and left me to complete their return. They now had a thorough understanding of the types of expenses they could and could not claim, and they said they were sending their friend to me to attend to his return as well.

Key points

- The settlement statement from your solicitor contains information needed for the preparation of your rental income and expenditure statement.

- The loan documentation will usually include details of the borrowing costs.

- Rental income is declared on a cash basis.

- Check real estate agent annual summaries against the monthly statements to satisfy yourself as to their accuracy.

- Capital and initial costs are not deductible.

- Repairs are claimable, but be clear about the distinction between repairs and improvements.

- Expenses inclusive of private use must be apportioned.

- Refer to appendix A for a checklist of deductible items.

Chapter 3

Variations of tax instalment deductions

Employers are required to withhold tax instalment deductions from wages paid to employees. The amount withheld is prescribed in a schedule provided by the Tax Office. The deductions are not a final tax liability. Rather, they are an estimation of tax that is applied as a credit against the tax as calculated on the employee's tax return.

The Taxation Commissioner has a discretion to allow a variation to the prescribed rates where an excessive credit will result at the end of the year. The Commissioner interprets this as where instalments would be the lesser of 10 per cent or $500 more than the amount owed.

This scenario is common to negatively geared properties. It is therefore possible to apply for a variation and obtain the tax benefits in your pay packet rather than wait until the end of the year and your tax refund.

The Tax Office will process an application if:

- It is able to identify your tax file number.
- You are up to date with your tax returns.
- You don't owe any tax.
- You have complied with your taxation obligations over the past three years.
- You don't have an existing provisional tax credit for the year in which you are applying.

A variation remains in force for only one year. A new application must be made each year if you want to continue the variation. If you change jobs during the year, or your circumstances change you need to make a fresh application.

I have never been keen on clients making applications for variations of tax instalment deductions. Human nature being what it is, most people will spend the extra money in their pay packets on day-to-day living. Receiving it as a lump sum in their tax refund gives them the ability to do something meaningful with the money, such as making a lump-sum payment off a loan, funding a holiday or purchasing a new lounge suite, to name a few.

Furthermore, I have seen many instances where clients, having purchased a rental property through a negative gearing promoter (who has then dutifully prepared an application that either underestimates income or overestimates expenditure), have found themselves facing an unexpected tax liability at tax return time. This can bring about a denial for a variation in the next year.

If you can't meet the loan payments without a tax instalment variation then you can't afford the property. Things are just too tight in that instance.

A sorry tale

Ray and Carol came to me on referral from a real estate agent. He had sold them a property at Edens Landing, south of Brisbane. I saw them late at night in my office. They were expecting a large refund but were soon disappointed. Both worked—Ray had a wage of $32 000 and Carol earned $30 000. On the advice of the agent the property had been acquired in Ray's name. Carol received a reasonable refund based on her normal income and deductions. But Ray, who incurred a loss of $6900 on his rental property, faced a liability of $1000. This had come about because of an incorrect variation application. If Ray had not had the variation, he would have received a refund close to $2500. It's no fun working back late and having to explain why he had to pay.

An accountant friend of mine is blunt about it. If his clients complain about a tax liability he comes straight out and asks why they believe they should be immune from paying tax—they earned the money, they have to pay tax on it. He then tells them to go and whinge to someone else because they won't get any sympathy from him, and cuts the discussion there.

I can't be that direct. To me, having to listen to the complaints is part of the job. But it is harder when the problem, such as the one just related, could have been avoided in the first place.

Chapter 4

The sale

Barry has been my client since the first year I started my practice. He was a plumber at the council until a heart attack forced him into an early retirement. At my suggestion, in 1986 Barry and his wife purchased a unit at the seaside town of Byron Bay. They paid $48 000 and it wasn't long before they had paid off the small loan taken out to finance it.

No longer working and having just reached pensionable age, Barry decided that it was time to sell the property. Because of the location and condition, it sold quickly. The $103 500 the couple received for it was earmarked for various things, but Barry was concerned about CGT liability.

He had maintained the relevant records and the calculation was simple (see tables 4.1 and 4.2 overleaf).

Table 4.1: the settlement statement for the purchase

Date of purchase	31 July 1986
Property cost	$48 000
Legal costs and stamp duty	$730

Table 4.2: the settlement statement for the sale

Date of purchase	19 March 2001
Property cost	$103 000
Legal costs and stamp duty	$700

A statement from the estate agent showed they earned a $4490 commission for this sale. No other costs had been incurred. Repairs had been attended to as required but no capital improvements had been made.

Two calculations need to be performed to see which CGT calculation option results in the smallest gain for tax purposes. These are illustrated in tables 4.3a, 4.3b and 4.4.

Table 4.3a: the frozen indexation method — calculation 1

Description of costs	Amt ($)	Date	Index factor	Indexed cost ($)
Property	48 000	31/7/86	1.59	76 320
Stamp duty and legals	730	31/7/86	1.59	1 161
Legal fees	700	19/03/01	1.00	700
Commission on sale	4 490	19/03/01	1.00	4 490
Cost base	53 920	**Frozen cost base**		82 671

Table 4.3b: the frozen indexation method — calculation 2

Consideration	$103 000
less frozen indexed cost base	$82 671
Capital gain	**$20 329**

Table 4.4: 50 per cent discount method

Consideration	$103000
less cost base	$53920
	$49080
less 50 per cent	$24540
Capital gain	**$24540**

In this instance, Barry and his wife elected to use the frozen indexation method (see table 4.5).

Table 4.5: capital gain apportioned

Barry	$10165
Jan	$10164
Total	**$20329**

Barry paid tax on the gain at his marginal rate of 31.5 per cent, as in table 4.6.

Table 4.6: capital gain with low-income offset

Taxable income	$10414.00
Tax thereon	$750.38
less low income offset	$150.00
Total tax	**$600.38**

Chapter 5

The goods and services tax

GST—what is it?

The goods and services tax (GST) is a tax on the consumption of goods and services. It is levied at a rate of 10 per cent of the price of most goods and services, and collected by the supplier of those goods and services. The law is encompassed in the *A New Tax System (Goods and Services Tax) Act 1999* and applied from 1 July 2000.

The effect on property

Goods and services tax applies to the construction of new homes and renovations. The price of those affected properties increased from 1 July 2000 to account for the tax. No GST is levied on the sale of property by a private individual.

Commercial properties

Goods and services tax applies to the construction, sale and renting of all non-residential land and buildings. This applies whether the properties are new or used. However, the owners of these properties act as tax collectors only and will be able to offset the tax charged to them against the tax collected. They are, though, required to remit the GST charged to the Commissioner of Taxation by the due date, which for everyone except large taxpayers is 21 October, January, April and July. This is for tax collected for the three-month periods ended 30 September, 31 December, 31 March and 30 June.

Residential rents

Goods and services tax is not charged on residential rents, providing that the lease will not continue for 50 years. Subject to the period of the lease spanning less than 50 years, these rents are classified as being input taxed. This term is described below.

Input taxed

The term 'input taxed' means that there is no entitlement to a credit for the tax paid on goods or services supplied. Costs incurred in the operating of a residential rental property are input taxed. This means an investor is not entitled to claim a credit for the tax on the costs of supplies—for example, repairs, body corporate fees, rates (excluding water and sewerage charges) and insurance—in respect of that property. However, this is not the case with business properties. If an investor owns a building that has a shop on the ground floor and a flat above, only the flat will be input taxed. The shop will be subject to GST.

The effect of GST

Because the costs of maintaining a residential rental property have increased as a result of GST, owners have been forced to either accept a lower return on their investment or increase the rent. This has not been the case with commercial premises, as, effectively, the owner pays no GST. Rather, he or she collects the tax from the business owner, who in turn offsets the tax paid against the tax collected from the goods he or she supplies to customers. However, it should be noted that unregistered persons (you do not have to register for GST if your taxable annual turnover is less than $50 000 per year) are not required to charge GST on their supplies and cannot claim credits for GST paid on their purchases.

Non-taxable supplies

There is no GST charged on interest, water and sewerage rates.

An example

John and Joy own a rental property at Marsden in Queensland. They are unable to increase the rents they charge because of an oversupply of properties in that area. They pay GST on the non-exempt costs incurred on their property. The GST component of those costs is deductible to the extent that the costs on which it is levied are allowable deductions.

A pre-GST and post-GST rental statement is set out in table 5.1 overleaf.

Table 5.1: effect of GST on rental property costs

Item	Pre-GST ($)	Post-GST ($)
Rent	7800	7800
less expenses		
Agents' fees	585	644
Bank charges	30	30
Borrowing costs	120	120
Cleaning	50	55
Decline in value	1200	1200
Pest control	90	99
Insurance	300	330
Interest	5200	5200
Rates	600	600
Repairs	600	660
Water and sewerage rates	140	140
	8915	9078
Net loss	**1115**	**1278**

Chapter 6

Capital gains tax and rental properties

Capital gains tax (CGT) applies to rental properties acquired after 19 September 1985. It is not a separate tax. The gain is calculated by taking the sale price and deducting from that the cost base of the property. The cost base comprises the original cost, incidental costs of acquisition, and the costs of transfer, improvements and sale.

If you acquired your rental property prior to 21 September 1999, you may choose to use the indexation method to determine the capital gain when you sell the property. This method indexes the cost base for inflation so that the taxable gain is the non-inflationary component. Indexation was frozen at 30 September 1999.

Alternatively, if you have owned the property as an individual for at least one year, you may elect to be taxed on half the non-indexed capital gain. A one-third CGT discount applies to superannuation funds. The discount is not available to companies. At the time of writing, the 50 per cent discount applies to trusts.

Indexation

Prior to the changes, the cost base of assets held for more than 12 months was indexed for inflation. This meant that tax was only paid on the non-inflationary component. Since the changes, the rules are as follows.

For all entities other than individuals and superannuation funds

If the property was acquired prior to 11.45 am on 21 September 1999 and you owned the property for more than 12 months prior to the disposal, you may choose to apply indexation up until 30 September 1999. From then on, indexation does not apply.

For individuals and superannuation funds

For properties owned prior to 11.45 am on 21 September 1999 you may elect to apply indexation up until 30 September 1999 or apply the CGT discount. If the property was acquired after 11.45 am on 21 September 1999 no indexation is available.

Table 6.1 sets out the indices to 30 September 1999.

The result of the removal of indexation is that, in times of high inflation, taxpayers who acquire rental properties for the long term will be worse off. This is because the longer they hold their assets, the more tax they will pay on the gain as a result of the inflation. This is illustrated in the example following table 6.1.

Table 6.1: capital gains tax indices September 1985 to September 1999

Year	March	June	September	December
1985			71.3	72.7
1986	74.4	75.6	77.6	79.8
1987	81.4	82.6	84.0	85.5
1988	87.0	88.5	90.2	92.0
1989	92.9	95.2	97.4	99.2
1990	100.9	102.5	103.3	106.0
1991	105.8	106.0	106.6	107.6
1992	107.6	107.3	107.4	107.9
1993	108.9	109.3	109.8	110.0
1994	110.4	111.2	111.9	112.8
1995	114.7	116.2	117.6	118.5
1996	119.0	119.8	120.1	120.3
1997	120.5	120.2	119.7	120.0
1998	120.3	121.0	121.3	121.9
1999	121.8	112.3	121.4	

An example

Adrian and Gail own a rental property on the Gold Coast. They purchased the property after 1 October 1999 for $300 000. Having bought well, but deciding they wanted to use their capital elsewhere, they sell the property five years later for $400 000. Ignoring the additional costs of purchase and sale, their gain is $100 000. Both Adrian and Gail are on a marginal tax rate of 46.5 per cent. During that period the consumer price index increased by 10 per cent. Tables 6.2 and 6.3 overleaf show how they are taxed.

Table 6.2: the old rules

Sale price	$400 000
less indexed cost base	
$300 000 x 1.10	$330 000
Taxable capital gain	$70 000
Tax at 46.5%	**$32 550**

Note: as their marginal tax rate is already 46.5 per cent, averaging will not apply.

Table 6.3: the current rules

Sale price	$400 000
less cost	$300 000
Capital gain	$100 000
less half the gain	$50 000
Taxable capital gain	$50 000
Tax at 46.5%	**$23 250**

Adrian and Gail will pay $9300 less GST in this example. But what if inflation rose 30 per cent in that time? See tables 6.4 and 6.5.

Table 6.4: the old rules with 30 per cent inflation

Sale price	$400 000
less indexed cost base	
$300 000 x 1.3	$390 000
Taxable capital gain	$10 000
Tax at 46.5%	**$4650**

Table 6.5: the current rules with 30 per cent inflation

Sale price	$400 000
less cost	$300 000
Capital gain	$100 000
less half the gain	$50 000
Taxable capital gain	$50 000
Tax at 46.5%	**$23 250**

There has been a real gain of $10 000, which has incurred tax of $23 250. Adrian and Gail are paying tax on an inflationary gain.

The effect on negative gearing

The rules may result in significant benefits for taxpayers on the 46.5 per cent tax rate who are fortunate enough to have their properties increase in value. For these people, the full gain will effectively be taxed at 23.25 per cent while they will have claimed a deduction for interest with a tax benefit of 46.5 per cent. Furthermore, those taxpayers not affected by the changes to prepaid expenses (business taxpayers with an annual turnover in excess of $1 million will no longer be able to claim prepayments) will still be able to pay up to 13 months of their interest and retain the immediate tax benefit.

From 13 May 1997 the indexed cost base of a property is reduced by the construction cost write-off. This only applies to properties acquired or improvements carried on after that date.

Removal of the averaging provisions

The averaging concessions which previously applied to individuals have been removed. Prior to 11.45 am on 21 September 1999, taxpayers with a capital gain of $27000 and no other income paid no tax. This has changed.

Mary had no income. She made a capital gain of $27000. As $27000 divided by 5 is $5400 and as that was the income tax threshold in the 2000 income year, she would have paid no tax. As a result of the changes, she would now pay tax on half of the gain (that is, $13500). At 2007 rates this would amount to $1125 tax payable.

Capital gains tax events

The general provision for determining the timing of a CGT event and its net capital gain or loss has been replaced by legislation that applies for each type of event. These events are the transactions that result in a capital gain or loss. Most times they relate to the sale or gifting of an asset and they apply to all CGT assets of Australian residents. Non-residents are only affected if the asset has a necessary connection with Australia (land, buildings and structures—including strata-title flats or home units—in Australia have a necessary connection). In addition, if you own shares in a company that owns a building on Australian land and gives you a right to occupy a flat or home unit in the building, those shares have the necessary connection.

With respect to property, a CGT event may occur upon:

* the sale of the property
* the gifting of the property

- a change in the beneficial ownership of the property

- an owner of the property ceasing to be an Australian resident.

The importance of timing

Your assessable income in any income year is affected by the timing of a CGT event. In respect of a rental property, the time of the event is the date of the contract. The timing of a gift of property is the date the gift was given. If you sign a contract in one income year and the property does not settle until the next, you should voluntarily include your capital gain in the year of signing the contract (even though settlement has not occurred). This way you will avoid having to lodge an amended return for the year after settlement. If settlement does not proceed there has not been a change in ownership and there is no CGT event, as there has not been a disposal.

If you use the indexation method and the consideration for the sale of property is between the cost base and the cost base after indexation, neither a capital gain nor loss occurs.

Method statement

The income tax legislation provides a method statement that must be followed in calculating the net gain or loss for an income year. It requires you to:

1 Calculate the current year's capital gains.

2 Deduct from this any current year's capital losses.

3 Deduct any prior years' unrecouped capital losses. This determines your notional net capital gain.

4 Deduct any applicable discount percentage. This determines your discount capital gain.

5 Deduct any small business concessions that may apply. The result will be your net capital gain.

The method statement requires that capital losses be applied against capital gains before the CGT discount is available.

It also provides procedures for calculating capital losses, namely:

- Calculate the sum of the capital losses for the year.

- Calculate the sum of the capital gains made during the year.

- Deduct the capital gains from the capital losses. If this provides an answer greater than zero, the result is the capital loss for the year.

Adrian has $1000 capital losses from prior years. He sells a rental property during the income year. He has owned the property for more than 12 months. He makes a profit of $10000 on the sale. During the year he lost $2000 from the sale of shares. His net capital gain is calculated in table 6.6.

Table 6.6: calculations for net capital gain

Current year's capital gains		$10000
less		
Current year's capital loss	$2000	
Prior year's capital loss	$1000	$3000
Notional net capital gain		$7000
less		
Discount percentage		$3500
Net capital gain		**$3500**

He must include the $3500 in his assessable income. This will be taxed at his marginal tax rate.

Improvements to a rental property that has been acquired prior to 19 September 1985 may be deemed as a separate asset. This will apply when:

- the building is demolished and a new one is constructed
- a property is constructed on vacant land
- adjacent land is purchased
- at the time of sale the indexed cost base of the improvement exceeds both

  1   5 per cent of the market value of the improved asset

  2   the limits set out in table 6.7

Table 6.7: threshold for assessing improvements as a separate asset

30 June	Threshold ($)	30 June	Threshold ($)
1986	50000	1995	82290
1987	53950	1996	84347
1988	58859	1997	88227
1989	63450	1998	89992
1990	68018	1999	89992
1991	73495	2000	91072
1992	78160	2001	92802
1993	80036	2002	97721
1994	80756		

I do not recommend the purchase of rental properties in companies. This is because at some time in the future, when a capital gain is distributed as a dividend, the indexation amount ends up being taxed (if applicable). This means that the whole capital gain will be taxed, not just the non-inflationary component. As well, there is no discount applied for rental properties owned by a company for more than 12 months. This means that there could be a minimum of 5.75 per cent extra tax because of the structure.

Don't dismiss the need to understand the effects of CGT. None of us knows what the future holds. It may well be that your circumstances change and, contrary to your previous intentions, you end up selling your rental investment.

Statistics (illustrated in figure 6.1, opposite) show that in the five years up to July 1997, 7.7 per cent of rental properties were sold to realise a capital gain. To break this down further, 4.9 per cent of former investors and 14.3 per cent of current investors sold for that reason. Until such time as a sale is made, any capital growth in a rental property is only a paper gain. It is not until it is sold that the profit (or loss) is realised.

Interestingly, 5.5 per cent sold to finance a purchase elsewhere. This suggests that a number of vendors may have become disillusioned with their investment, wanted to improve the quality of their residence or sought shelter from potential CGT liability in the future (in the tax-exempt haven of their principal residence).

Another group, 10.2 per cent of investors, sold because they considered there was an inadequate return on their investment, and 9.2 per cent couldn't afford to keep it.

Figure 6.1: reasons for selling in five years to June 1997

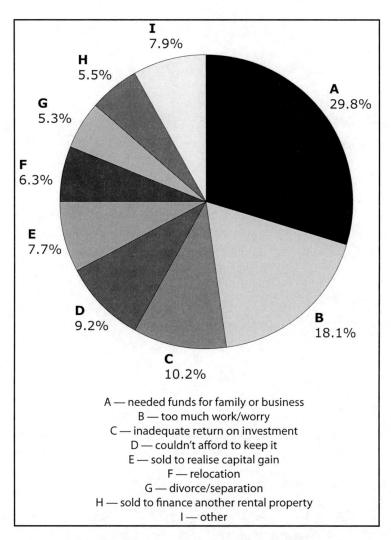

I
7.9%

H
5.5%

G
5.3%

F
6.3%

E
7.7%

A
29.8%

D
9.2%

B
18.1%

C
10.2%

A — needed funds for family or business
B — too much work/worry
C — inadequate return on investment
D — couldn't afford to keep it
E — sold to realise capital gain
F — relocation
G — divorce/separation
H — sold to finance another rental property
I — other

Source of data: Australian Bureau of Statistics publication
Household Investors in Rental Dwellings Australia, June 1997

Chapter 7

Decline in value revisited

Decline in value is a term used to describe the amortisation of the cost of an asset over its effective life. A deduction is allowed if the asset can be classified as plant or articles (see the following pages), is owned by the taxpayer and is used to produce assessable income during the year, or is installed ready for use.

As previously mentioned, there are two methods acceptable for use for tax purposes. These are the diminishing value method and the prime cost method.

The diminishing value method calculates depreciation as a percentage of the asset's depreciated value (see table 7.1 overleaf). The prime cost method calculates depreciation as a percentage of the asset's cost (see table 7.2 overleaf). The diminishing value rate is 2.0 times the prime cost rate. For assets purchased before 10 May 2006, the rate is 1.5 times the prime cost rate.

Table 7.1: example of diminishing value method

Furniture cost	$1 000
Written-down value 01/07/07	$800
Depreciation at 15%	$120
Written-down value 30/06/08	**$680**

Table 7.2: example of prime cost method

Furniture cost	$1 000
Written-down value 01/07/07	$800
Depreciation at 7.5%	$60
Written-down value 30/06/08	**$740**

The diminishing value basis has the advantage of providing a higher deduction in the initial years, therefore resulting in less tax in those years. The prime cost method (with the exception of part-year claims) offers the advantage of enabling an equal write-off in each year.

An item must be owned by the taxpayer to qualify for the claim. This means, for example, that you can't claim for the decline in value on a refrigerator owned by your tenant.

Definition of plant or articles

On 24 November 2004, the Tax Office issued a ruling, TR 2004, dealing with the definition of plant in residential rental properties. Prior to this, although there were rulings that could be used as checklists for determining whether an item was depreciable plant, the tables in the rulings were far from exhaustive and some items were difficult to classify. For example, the courts have determined that kitchen cupboards do not constitute plant, yet not so long ago they were generally considered depreciable.

When claiming decline in value on an item of plant, consideration must be given as to whether the article is used to produce income or is part of the house or land. To illustrate, a concrete swimming pool would not considered plant but a filtration plant would.

Effective life rates

The decline in value for plant and equipment acquired after 1 September 1999 is determined by the effective life of the asset. The effective life may be determined by you (using the guidelines outlined in the Australian Taxation Office publication *Guide to Depreciation*—NAT 7170) or from advisory rates established by the Commissioner of Taxation. Those advisory rates are contained in the following tax rulings:

- IT 2685, effective to 1 January 2001
- TR 2000/18, effective from 1 January 2001
- TR 2000/18CD.

Table 7.3 shows the effective life for rental property assets from rulings IT 2685 and TR2000/18.

The decline in value rate to be claimed is calculated in table 7.4, which begins on page 54.

Table 7.3: the effective life for rental property assets from rulings IT 2685 and TR2000/18

| Item | Effective life in years given in | |
	IT 2685	TR 2000/18
Air-conditioning		
—room units	15	13.33
Alarms	20	20
Blinds, venetian	20	20
Carpet	10	10
Curtains and drapes	7	6.66
Electric bed	15	13.33
Electric clock	15	13.33
Electric heater	10	10
Furniture and fittings	15	13.33
Garbage unit,		
compacting	7	6.66
Hot-water service	20	20
Lawnmowers		
—motor	7	6.66
—self-propelled	5	5
Linoleum and similar		
floor coverings	10	10
Microwave ovens	7	6
Radios	10	10
Refrigerators	15	13.33
Stoves	20	20
Television sets	10	10
Vacuum cleaners	10	10
Washing machines	7	6.66

Diminishing value method

Pre–10 May 2006 acquisitions

$$\text{Opening written-down value} \times \left(\frac{\text{Days owned}}{\text{Days in the year}} \right) \times \left(\frac{150\%}{\text{Effective life}} \right)$$

Post–9 May 2006 acquisitions

$$\text{Opening written-down value} \times \left(\frac{\text{Days owned}}{\text{Days in the year}} \right) \times \left(\frac{200\%}{\text{Effective life}} \right)$$

Prime cost method

$$\text{Cost} \times \left(\frac{\text{Days owned}}{\text{Days in the year}} \right) \times \left(\frac{100\%}{\text{Effective life}} \right)$$

Dividing by the prescribed effective life adds needless complication. It makes more sense to use the percentage rates as follows over the page in tables 7.4 and 7.5 (calculated using the Commissioner's formula) and apply these in your calculation.

Table 7.4: IT 2685 rates

Item	Rates Prime cost %	Diminishing value %
Air-conditioning		
—room units	6.67	10
Alarms	5	5
Blinds, venetian	5	7.5
Carpet	10	15
Curtains and drapes	14.285	21.43
Electric bed	6.67	10
Electric clock	6.67	10
Electric heater	10	15
Furniture and fittings	6.67	10
Garbage unit, compacting	14.285	21.43
Hot-water service	5	7.5
Lawnmowers		
—motor	14.285	21.43
—self-propelled	20	20
Linoleum and similar		
floor coverings	10	15
Microwave ovens	14.285	21.43
Radios	10	15
Refrigerators	6.67	10
Stoves	5	7.5
Television sets	10	15
Vacuum cleaners	10	15
Washing machines	14.285	21.43

Table 7.5: TR 2000/18 rates

Item	Prime cost %	Rates Diminishing value % Pre–10 May 2006 purchase	Post–9 May 2006 purchase
Air-conditioning			
— room units	6.67	10	13.34
Alarms	5	5	10
Blinds, venetian	5	7.5	10
Carpet	10	15	20
Curtains and drapes	15	22.5	30
Electric bed	7.5	11.25	15
Electric clock	7.5	11.25	15
Electric heater	10	15	20
Furniture and fittings	7.5	11.25	15
Garbage unit, compacting	15	22.5	30
Hot-water service	5	7.5	10
Lawnmowers (motor)	15	22.5	30
Lawnmowers (self-propelled)	20	30	40
Linoleum and similar floor coverings	10	15	20
Microwave ovens	15	22.5	30
Radios	10	15	20
Refrigerators	7.5	11.25	15
Stoves	5	7.5	10
Television sets	10	15	20
Vacuum cleaners	10	15	20
Washing machines	15	22.5	30

Table 7.6 shows the effective life and decline in value rates from information drawn from the Tax Office guidelines.

Table 7.6: decline in value — effective life and rates

Asset	Effective life (years)	Prime cost %	Diminishing value %	
			Pre–10 May 2006 purchase	Post–9 May 2006 purchase
Air-conditioning				
— room units	6.67	10	13.34	20
— packaged	15	6.67	10	30
Barbecues (freestanding)	6	20	30	12
Blinds (internal)	10	10	15	20
Carpet	10	10	15	20
Cassette players	7	14.29	21.43	14
Ceiling fans	5	20	30	10
Clocks (electric)	10	10	15	20
Closed circuit				
— cameras	4	25	37.5	50
— monitors	4	25	37.5	50
Clothes dryers	10	10	15	20
CD players	7	14.29	21.43	14
Cook tops	12	8.33	12.5	16.66
Cordless phones	4	25	37.5	50
Crockery and cutlery	5	20	30	40
Curtains	6	16.67	25	33.34
Dishwashers	10	10	15	20
Door closers and stops	10	10	15	20
DVD players	5	20	30	40

Decline in value revisited

Asset	Effective life (years)	Prime cost %	Diminishing value %	
			Pre–10 May 2006 purchase	Post–9 May 2006 purchase
Electric gates				
—control	5	20	30	40
—motors	10	10	15	20
Electric heaters	15	6.67	10	13.34
Emergency warning sys.	12	8.33	12.5	16.66
Evap. cooling				
—fixed	20	5	7.5	10
—portable	10	10	15	20
Exhaust fans	10	10	15	20
Fire alarms	6	16.67	25	33.34
Fire extinguishers	15	6.67	10	13.34
Floating timber flooring	15	6.67	10	13.34
Freezers	12	8.33	12.5	16.66
Furniture	13	7.5	11.25	15
Garage door				
—motors	10	10	10	10
—controls	5	20	30	40
Garbage bins	10	10	15	20
Garbage disposal units	10	10	15	20
Garden lights (solar)	8	12.5	7.5	25
Garden sheds (freestanding)	15	6.7	10	13.34
Garden watering systems	5	20	30	40

Table 7.6 *(cont'd)*: decline in value — effective life and rates

| Asset | Effective life (years) | Prime cost % | Diminishing value % | |
			Pre–10 May 2006 purchase	Post–9 May 2006 purchase
Gas central heat. (ducted)	20	5	7.5	10
Gas heaters	15	6.67	10	13.34
Generators	15	6.67	10	13.34
Hand dryers (electrical)	10	10	15	20
Hot-water sys. — electric and gas	12	8.33	12.5	16.66
— solar	15	6.67	10	13.34
Intercom	10	10	15	20
Ironing boards	7	14.29	21.43	28.58
Irons	5	20	30	40
Lighting	5	20	30	40
Linen	5	20	30	40
Linoleum and vinyl floor coverings	10	10	15	20
Microwave ovens	10	10	15	20
Mirrors (freestanding)	15	6.67	10	13.34
Outdoor carpet	5	20	30	40
Ovens	12	8.33	12.5	16.66
Pergola louvre (controls and motors)	15	6.67	10	13.34

Decline in value revisited

Asset	Effective life (years)	Prime cost %	Diminishing value %	
			Pre–10 May 2006 purchase	Post–9 May 2006 purchase
Pumps	25	4	6	8
Radios	10	10	15	20
Range hoods	12	8.33	12.5	16.66
Refrigerators	12	8.33	12.5	16.66
Rugs	7	14.29	21.43	28.58
Sauna heating	15	6.7	10	13.34
Security systems				
— code pads	5	20	30	40
— control panels	5	20	30	40
Spa bath				
— chlorinators	12	8.33	12.5	16.66
— filtration units	12	8.33	12.5	16.66
— heaters	15	6.67	10	13.34
— freestanding	17	5.88	8.82	11.76
Stoves	12	8.33	12.5	16.66
Surround sound systems	20	5	7.5	10
Swimming pool				
— chlorinators	12	8.33	12.5	16.66
— filtration units	12	8.33	12.5	16.66
— heaters (gas and electricity)	15	6.67	10	13.34
— heaters (solar)	20	5	7.5	10
Telephones	10	10	15	20

Table 7.6 *(cont'd)*: decline in value — effective life and rates

Asset	Effective life (years)	Prime cost %	Diminishing value %	
			Pre–10 May 2006 purchase	Post–9 May 2006 purchase
TV antennas (freestanding)	5	20	30	40
TV sets	10	10	15	20
Vacuum cleaners	10	10	15	20
Ventilation fans	20	5	7.5	10
Video cassette recorders	5	20	30	40
Washing machines	10	10	15	20
Water filters	15	6.67	10	13.34
Water pumps	20	5	7.5	10

At last, the ATO has given guidance as to the effective life of items such as dishwashers, extractor fans, light fittings, removable range hoods and other common rental-property depreciable items. Taxpayers no longer have to determine the effective life of these assets.

The rates to use

Items purchased prior to 11:45 am on 21 September 1999 may continue to be depreciated at the accelerated depreciation rates in force at that time. These rates were published in the first edition of *Rental Property and Taxation*. For plant acquired after 11:45 am on 21 September 1999 but before 1 January 2001, the effective life estimates should be made with reference to

IT 2685. For plant acquired from 1 January 2001, the effective life estimates should be made with reference to TR 2000/18. For plant acquired after 1 July 2004, the current rates should be used.

Non-depreciable items

It is important to ensure that the asset being amortised is not regarded as part of the property (the setting)—it must be an item of plant. For this reason, the following items (this list is not exhaustive) will form part of the cost used for claiming the special building write-off rather than being available for depreciation.

Capital works items

- air-conditioning ducting, pipes and vents
- automatic garage doors (excluding controls and motors)
- barbeques (fixed)
- bathroom accessories (fixed)
- bathroom fixtures
- bollards (fixed)
- car parks (sealed)
- carports
- clotheslines
- cupboards (other than freestanding)
- door locks and latches
- door stops (fixed)
- driveways (sealed)
- electrical conduits, switchboards, distribution boards, power points and wiring
- facades (fixed)
- fencing
- fire doors and separation
- fireplaces
- floor coverings (fixed)
- furniture (other than freestanding)

- garage doors
- garbage chutes
- garden awnings and shade structures
- garden lights (fixed)
- garden sheds (other than freestanding)
- garden watering installations
- gates
- grease traps
- hand rails
- heating ducts, pipes, vents and wiring
- hot-water system piping
- hydrants
- insulation
- jetties and boat sheds
- kitchen fixtures (bench tops, cupboards, sinks, tapware and tiles)
- laundry fixtures
- letter boxes
- lift wells
- light fittings (hard-wired)
- master antenna television

- mirrors (fixed)
- operable pergola louvers (excluding controls and motors)
- paths
- ramps
- retaining walls
- safes (fixed)
- sanitary fixtures (fixed)
- satellite dishes
- saunas
- septic tanks
- sewerage treatment assets (excluding controls and motors)
- security doors and screens
- shelving (fixed)
- showers
- shutters
- signs (fixed)
- skylights
- spa baths (excluding pumps)
- spas (fixed assets)
- sprinkler systems
- swimming pools

- television antennas (fixed)
- tennis courts (including fences, lights, posts and surfaces)
- vacuum cleaners (ducted)
- ventilation ducting and vents
- wardrobes

- water piping
- water tanks
- window awnings, insect screens, louvers, pelmets and tracks
- window shutters.

Care must be taken to review the deductibility of items included in a quantity surveyor's report, and the rates used. These professionals are qualified to apportion values as to the cost, not to make decisions as to whether the items are rightfully included on a decline in value schedule (see appendix D for an example).

It is your responsibility to ensure that the item is depreciable and that the applied rate can be justified. A quantity surveyor does not have the qualifications to do this.

I often come across non-applicable items on such schedules and have many times witnessed the use of incorrect rates. In one instance, I challenged a high-profile firm of surveyors who had included non-applicable items in a report that they prepared for a client of mine. When they persisted in arguing they were right, I asked whether they had anyone with tax qualifications on their staff. Their answer was no. Two months later, they sent my client a letter offering to prepare, for a cost of $60, an amended report to comply with changes to the income tax laws. There had been no changes. I wonder how many people paid the fee. My client didn't.

In another instance, a new client had lodged a previous return based on a quantity surveyor's figures. The Tax Office adjusted the return. The surveyors (again, a high profile firm) refused to accept responsibility. My client decided the costs of pursuing the matter were too great. Hopefully, if you are using an accountant to prepare your return, he or she will adjust any inaccurate schedules.

Replacement basis

Since 1 July 2000, taxpayers have not been able to claim the cost of items such as crockery and linen on a replacement basis. Items such as these must either be depreciated, included as part of a low-value pool, or written off under the provision that allows an immediate deduction for plant costing less than $301 (see below).

Items costing less than $301

An immediate write-off for items costing $300 or less is available for non-business taxpayers.

However, there is no deduction available for the immediate write-off of an asset that costs less than $301 and that is part of a set of assets.

The ATO has issued a fact sheet disclosing its guidelines on how to apply the write-off (*Non-business depreciating assets costing $300 or less*—NAT 7284-7.2002).

The claim is available when all of the following conditions are met:

1   The asset is used more than 50 per cent of the time in the production of non-business income.

2   It is not part of a set of assets acquired in the same income year where the total cost of the set is greater than $300.

3   It is not one of a number of identical (or substantially identical) assets the total cost of which, in the same income year, exceeds $300.

Items failing this test must either be depreciated separately over their effective life or as part of a low-value pool.

The immediate write-off must be reduced to account for any private use, if applicable.

An asset may be part of a set if it is interdependent on the other assets, marketed as a set, or designed to be used together.

Assets are deemed to be identical if they are:

- the same in all respects
- the same but for some minor or incidental differences.

If a rental property is owned in joint names, the $300 applies to each owner. That is, if an asset costs $600 and the property is owned 50/50 by joint owners, each owner can claim the $300 immediately. The asset does not have to be amortised under the decline in value rules. This is because the $300 claim is applied to each owner's joint interest in the asset.

The Tax Act provides that if an asset is held jointly (except assets held by a partnership carrying on a business), each joint owner's interest in the asset is treated as the depreciating asset.

Low-value pooling

An option exists for individual items of plant costing less than $1000 and acquired after 1 July 2000 to be placed in a low-value pool. Items held in the previous year of income with a written-down value of less than $1000 may also be placed in the pool. This pool is then depreciated using the diminishing value method at the two following statutory rates:

1 18.75 per cent for items allocated to the pool for the first time in the income year

2 37.5 per cent for plant allocated to the pool in a previous income year and low written-down value items added to the pool in the current year of income.

If you elect to use pooling, all other low-cost items acquired in that year and later income years must be allocated to the pool.

Should pooling be used?

Many rental property depreciable assets have an effective life of over four years. At the same time, many have a cost of less than $1000. As items in the pool are effectively written-off over four years (at the 37.5 per cent rate), pooling provides an attractive alternative because of the resulting higher depreciation claim in the initial years.

Example

The examples set out in tables 7.7 and 7.8 assume the rental property assets were purchased on 1 January 2001.

Table 7.7: capital allowance claim without pooling

Asset	Date acquired	Cost $	Diminish. value rate %	Decline in value $	Undeduct. cost $
Carpets	01/01/01	2500	15	187	2313
Curtains	01/01/01	2000	22.5	225	1775
Hot-water system	01/01/01	800	7.5	30	770
Stove	01/01/01	600	7.5	22	578
				464	

Table 7.8: capital allowance claim with pooling

Asset	Date acquired	Cost $	Diminish. value rate %	Decline in value $	Undeduct. cost $
Carpets	01/01/01	2 500	15	187	2313
Curtains	01/01/01	2 000	22.5	225	1775
				412	

Pooling		
Opening pool balance 01/01/01		$0
Additions to pool in 2001		
Hot-water system	$800	
Stove	$600	
	$1 400	
Depreciation at 18.75%	$263	**$1 137**

Pooling	
Closing pool balance 30/06/01	$1 137
Depreciation as per schedule	$412
Depreciation as per pool	$263
Depreciation claim	**$675**

In this example, the landlord obtains a claim greater by $211 by utilising pooling. In the next year the advantage will be even greater as the rate used for the pooled assets will be 37.5 per cent.

Private use

An apportionment must be made for private use when a depreciable asset is not used solely for income-producing purposes. This is of particular relevance to holiday units that may be occupied by the owner for part of the year.

Disposal of assets

When depreciation has been claimed on an item and the item is sold or otherwise disposed of, a balancing adjustment needs to be made. If the item is sold for less than the written-down value, the resulting loss is deductible in the year of sale. If a profit is made, the difference is assessable income.

Conversely, in the event that an item that was part of a low-value pool is sold, the pool's closing balance for the year of disposal is reduced by the sale price. However, in this instance, there is no need to adjust the depreciation for the number of days the asset was held during the year because the asset is still eligible for a full year's claim.

Take care

In its publication, *1997 Tax Returns Desktop Guide*, the Centre for Professional Development advises that, when preparing a depreciation schedule, care should be taken to ensure:

- the opening written-down values equal the closing written down values of the previous year

- additions and disposals are shown in separate columns

- each column adds downwards and cross-adds to the closing written-down value as follows:

  Written-down value + additions – disposals +or- adjustments on disposal = value for depreciation – depreciation = closing written-down value

- private use is deducted

- an adjustment is made to apportion the depreciation for assets acquired or disposed of during the year—this should be on a daily basis.

Chapter 8

Construction cost write-off

A special write-off applies for the construction cost of residential income-producing buildings where construction commenced after 18 July 1985. A claim is also available for structural improvements made after 27 February 1992. The costs are deductible as shown in table 8.1.

Table 8.1: construction cost deductions

Construction cost	% rate	Years
18/07/85–15/09/87	4.0	25
15/09/87–	2.5	40

The construction costs include:

• architects' fees

• surveying

- engineering

- building approval fees

- cost of construction

- cost of foundation excavations

- cost of fencing

- cost of retaining walls

- in-ground swimming pools.

They exclude:

- land costs

- demolition of existing structure

- site preparation prior to excavation works

- landscaping

- items deductible under other sections of the Tax Act.

Where the costs cannot be precisely determined, the Tax Office will accept estimates by a quantity surveyor, clerk of works, supervising architect or an experienced builder. The Commissioner will not accept estimates from valuers, real estate agents, solicitors or accountants.

The deduction is calculated from the day the building is first used after completion of construction. However, it is only available in respect of periods where the building is used or maintained ready for rental.

As discussed previously, construction cost write-offs for properties acquired after the 1997 Budget reduced the cost base for CGT purposes. This may have a significant effect on the taxation of profits on rental properties sold in the future. This adjustment must be made even if a claim for the allowance has not.

Chapter 9

Interest

Interest is often the most significant claim made against rental income. In June 1997, the Tax Office wrote to taxpayers who had made high rental interest claims. They were concerned that many taxpayers made errors in their claims for interest deductions. This led to an increase in the number of rental audits. The department identified seven key 'points people need to think about when claiming rental interest deductions'. These were:

1   Interest on funds borrowed for private purposes is not deductible. The use of the borrowed money determines the deductibility of the interest, not the security provided.

2   Interest should be apportioned on a loan used both for private and rental purposes. Only the rental portion should be claimed.

3   Where rental properties are in joint names, interest must generally be split in accordance with the legal ownership of the property 'and not claimed solely by the income-earning partner's'.

4   In domestic arrangements interest deductions may be limited. Where there is a non–arms-length rental at a non-commercial rent, the deduction should be calculated on a 'pro rata basis or limited to the amount of actual rent received'.

5   Advance payments towards the principal of a loan are not deductible. However, provided the interest debt has become due and liable to the lender and the interest is for a period of less than 13 months, interest in advance will normally be deductible.

6   Unless the loan is interest-only, repayments are made up of both interest and principal. Only the interest can be claimed.

7   The Tax Office does not accept that investors are entitled to the extra deductions obtained from linked, split or accelerator loans, and will allow a deduction only to the extent of that to which you would be entitled to 'under a traditional loan arrangement'. This view has been confirmed by the courts.

I doubt that many of the above problems would have related to returns prepared by tax agents (provided that all the necessary information was given to the agent, that is). The law is reasonably clear on the deductibility of interest and there really isn't any excuse when a taxpayer gets it wrong.

So, to minimise any tax audit query, it is important to keep clear and accurate records in respect to each loan. The loan bank statements should be set aside in a safe place, as the interest may be possibly the largest deduction you will need to verify.

Interest is deductible when it becomes due and payable. Hence the Commissioner's concern with interest prepayments. It is important to ensure that, when an up-front payment is made, the payment is for interest, and that there is no principal component involved. This may not be possible under the loan conditions—check with your bank before making an early payment. See table 9.1 for an example of the reduction in tax payable when an up-front interest payment is made.

Effect of an up-front interest payment

Assumptions

Loan: $120 000 principal—interest at 9.3 per cent with the right to make payments of interest in advance

Prepay: 12 months' interest

Interest prepaid: $11 160

Table 9.1: tax reduction from an up-front interest payment

Marginal tax rate including Medicare levy	Reduction in tax
16.5%	$1 953.00
31.5%	$3 515.40
41.5%	$4 631.40
46.5%	$5 189.40

Line of credit facilities

It has become common in recent times for lending institutions to offer lines of credit and loans with redraw facilities. You must be aware of the need to apportion the private and rental property components of these arrangements. The private component is non-deductible and cannot be claimed. The interest applicable to the rental remains deductible.

Accurate records must be maintained when you make deposits and withdrawals from these accounts. In some of these arrangements, the rental property owner's salary is paid directly into the line of credit account. The owner pays most of his or her expenses by credit card. The credit card is then repaid out of the line of credit account. This is a useful strategy for loans on which the interest is not tax-deductible.

However, I have seen instances where a taxpayer's only borrowings are against his or her rental property and this strategy has been used. This causes a tax problem, where eventually the majority of the loan will change from an investment loan to a private one. Each payment of personal credit card debts from the redraw facility becomes a new borrowing of funds. As the purpose is to repay a non-deductible credit card debt, the interest on the new borrowing is not deductible. This means that, each time this happens, the income-producing portion of the loan must be calculated.

Loans with standard redraw facility

A recent case has highlighted the danger of mixing investment and private borrowings in a personal savings account. In *Domjan v FC* [2004] ATC 2204 it was held that interest was not deductible despite the funds having been originally used to purchase rental properties.

The taxpayers in question had a joint loan account that was used to purchase three rental properties between 1992 and 1999. In 1999, one property was sold to the taxpayers' sons.

The proceeds were used to fund part of the taxpayers' interest in the third rental property, which was acquired in the same month. Funds from the sale of shares and a drawdown from the joint loan account were also used to fund the acquisition. Salary direct deposits were made to the joint account over a number of years, as well as repayments of funds in excess of the minimum bank requirements.

Between 1996 and 1999, withdrawals were made from the loan account for both income and non–income-producing purposes. The redrawn funds were deposited in a personal savings account before being applied to the purpose for which they were drawn. This meant the monies were mixed with funds already in the savings account.

A deduction was claimed for interest incurred on the joint loan because one of the taxpayers contended the monies were originally used for income-producing purposes. She argued that, when she made the redraws, she was accessing her own private funds. She believed the excess repayments to the loan account were the same as depositing private funds into a bank account. She argued the purpose of the original borrowings remained intact.

The Tax Office disagreed. It disallowed the interest claims because:

1   Each redraw was a new borrowing and the deductibility is dependent on the basis of what was done with the funds.

2   Once the redraws were intermingled with other funds in the savings account, it was impossible to determine the source of each withdrawal from that account. It followed that it could not determine the extent to which interest paid on the redraws was related to income-producing investment.

The Administrative Appeals Tribunal agreed with the Tax Office, rejecting the taxpayers' argument. The result was that no part of the interest in respect of the redrawn funds was an allowable deduction.

Chapter 10

Interest-only loans: a strategy

I previously mentioned that, in general, I don't believe interest-only money to be an appropriate form of finance in a low-inflation economy. However, I would be remiss not to relate the following to you.

In 1998, Brian purchased a house in Rochedale South (a suburb in Logan City, close to Brisbane) for $115 000. He decided to finance the property with an interest-only loan over five years. He was on the highest marginal tax rate and decided that he would use gearing to attempt to maximise the creation of his net wealth. Brian had a number of other investments and the ability to save around $100 per week. Furthermore, he had some cash tucked away in a cash management trust.

Brian's wife doesn't work and he decided to invest $400 per month in an imputation fund in her name. The imputation credits from the money earned would offset any tax liability incurred by his spouse. He intends to continue to do this over the next 10 years and to reinvest all distributions back in the fund.

The effect of this is interesting. If the fund earns 16 per cent per year at the end of 10 years he will have amassed around $117 000 and be able to repay the loan in full.

If he had taken a principal and interest loan at 6.7 per cent p.a. over 20 years, his repayments would have been $871 per month. If, instead of investing the $400 per month in the imputation fund, he paid the extra off the loan, at the end of 10 years there would still be $8000 outstanding on the loan. Monthly payments of $1318 would be required to repay the loan in full in that time.

However, things may not work out this way. There is no guarantee he will continue to invest the $400 per month and the sums change dramatically if the fund does not perform as hoped. If a return of 10 per cent is achieved, he will have $82 000 available to reduce the loan, leaving a balance of $33 000 outstanding — a far cry from his present thinking.

The reality is that most people will not use this type of strategy. Or, if they do, they will stay with it for a short time only. Few of us have the discipline to see such a plan through.

Chapter 11

Split loans

A split loan exists where money is borrowed and allocated between two accounts—one for personal purposes and the other for investment. The lender establishes the payments required to pay off the loan over a set period and repayments are then allocated against the private account. Interest is capitalised against the investment account until such time as the private account is repaid. Repayments are then directed to the investment account. See table 11.1 on page 84 for an example of the repayment of a split loan.

If this was effective for tax purposes it would provide a tax benefit. A bigger deduction would be available than would have been if the arrangement had not been entered into.

Success in the Spotless case, detailed below, gave the Tax Office the authority to take a wider view of the anti-avoidance legislation contained in the Tax Act. As a result, split loans came under attack.

In the Spotless case, the taxpayer invested monies offshore to take advantage of a tax benefit. The High Court found that this was the dominant purpose for making the investment and that the anti-avoidance legislation should apply.

Recognising that any challenge to a split loan arrangement would be unlikely to succeed under the general deduction provisions of the Tax Act, the department decided to apply Part IVA (the anti-avoidance powers). They believed it applied because with split loans:

- there is a scheme

- a tax benefit flows from that scheme

- the scheme is entered into with the dominant purpose of gaining a tax benefit.

As previously mentioned in chapter 9, in an information letter mailed to taxpayers who owned rental properties in June 1997, the Tax Office made it clear that it did not accept the extra interest deductions thought to result from 'linked loans, split loans or accelerator loans'. It also stated that it would only allow a deduction equal to the amount of a taxpayer's entitlement under a traditional loan arrangement.

It had been argued that the purpose of split loans is to increase wealth through cash flow management and property investment, and that the private account is repaid before the investment account because the interest on the private account is not deductible. The contrasting argument is that this is a normal commercial decision and not the same as entering into a scheme to obtain a tax benefit. Therefore, it was countered, Part IVA does not apply.

The Commissioner of Taxation issued Taxation Ruling 98/22, which applies to those loan facilities where:

1   A taxpayer borrows money and the loan is allocated between two or more accounts.

2   At least one of the accounts is for private purposes and the other for income-producing purposes.

3   The borrower makes repayments only against the private account until it is repaid and payments are then made against the other account.

In the Commissioner's opinion, there is no commercial explanation for incurring the extra interest amount on the income-producing loan. He considers such arrangements as being organised so as to reduce the principal on the non–income-producing loan and that the extra interest (the capitalised interest) on the other loan is non-deductible.

He comes to the conclusion that the interest on the investment account must be apportioned between the deductible and non-deductible amounts.

The Commissioner comments that if a taxpayer disposes of the income-producing asset tied to the facility, the capitalised interest is not a cost of ownership for CGT cost base calculation purposes.

In *FCT v Hart & Anor* ATC 4599, the High Court confirmed the Tax Office's view. In this case, taxpayers were denied a deduction for the additional interest incurred through the accrual of interest on the investment portion of a split loan arrangement. Their claim was limited to the interest they would have paid if they had entered into a normal loan agreement. This does not mean there is no deduction allowed when interest compounds. The Federal Court found that normal interest and compound interest are both deductible according to the use to which the borrowings are put. However, the High Court found that the anti-avoidance provisions of the legislation applied and denied the deduction. It was decided that the dominant purpose for entering into the split loan arrangement was to obtain the tax benefit ostensibly obtained with it.

Prior to the High Court's decision, some advisers were suggesting that a claim should be made for the interest on interest. This was despite Hart's case (where the taxpayer had succeeded in the Federal Court) having been appealed to the High Court. When the decision was handed down, the ATO advised that taxpayers who had claimed all of the interest under a split loan arrangement could request an amendment.

If voluntary disclosure was made, the penalty imposed would be remitted to 5 per cent of the tax shortfall (plus general interest charge). Although a substantially higher penalty could have been applied, this highlights the need for caution when taking an aggressive tax position.

Table 11.1: example of a split loan

	Interest ($)	Repayment ($)	Balance ($)
Investment account			
1 July 2000			120000
31 July 2000	682		120682
31 August 2000	687		121369
30 September 2000	668		122037
Private account			
1 July 2000			100000
31 July 2000	569	1000	99569
31 August 2000	563	1600	98532
30 September 2000	539	1600	97471

Chapter 12

Negative gearing

The question most frequently asked by my clients when considering the purchase of a rental property is 'What is negative gearing?' Most of them have heard of it but few understand it. For some reason they feel it is the Holy Grail that will help them reduce their tax. It may, but at what cost? It can be a high-risk strategy that will magnify both losses and gains over time. It has its place and is most useful to a taxpayer on the highest marginal rate. But the sums should be done before entering into a negatively geared arrangement. Is the risk worth the gain? Handled sensibly, it may be. But don't just blindly accept it as the right thing to do.

As mentioned previously, gearing is a term that refers to the amount of borrowing. For example, if your loans accounted for 90 per cent of your investment worth, you would be said to be highly geared. If they totalled 10 per cent, the gearing would be low.

Negative gearing occurs when interest on borrowings to finance an income-producing asset produces a tax loss. That tax loss can be offset against income from other sources and results in a reduction of tax payable.

There is a chance of a property becoming vacant and remaining unlet for a long period of time. Mortgage commitments will still have to be met. If you are dependent on the rental income to fund the loan, you may find yourself getting behind with the repayments. Eventually you may be forced to sell the property, perhaps for significantly less than you paid, resulting in a loss of money.

Don't pass that off lightly—it has happened before and will, no doubt, happen again.

This highlights the often unconsidered fact that negative gearing creates a shortfall. Although that shortfall may, in part, be funded by the Tax Office, the balance has to be found from after-tax income. If the after-tax income is insufficient to meet the need, the result can be disastrous.

It is important to consider Taxation Ruling TR 95/33. Here the Commissioner expresses his opinion that, if the disproportion between the assessable income and the outgoing is to derive a tax deduction, the outgoing will be partially or wholly disallowed.

In other words, from the start, the taxpayer should intend that the losses eventually will become positive. If this is not the intention, then the earning of assessable income may not be his or her only motive in entering the transaction, and the interest deduction may be adjusted. This has even more significance since the finding in the Spotless case referred to earlier (see page 82).

Why negative gear if the loss created is not offset by the increase in the value of the rental property? The purpose of any investment should be to create wealth, not destroy it.

Table 12.1 shows an example of the after-tax loss, at the top marginal tax rate, of a negatively geared property. The loss of $2140 is the amount that has to be found to finance the loss after the tax benefit has been received.

Table 12.1: after-tax loss on a negatively geared property

Negative gearing loss	$4000
Tax at 46.5% (with Medicare levy)	$1860
Net loss after tax	**$2140**

If the property value was constant, there would be a net reduction of wealth of $2140. If the property value decreased, the reduction would be the sum of the after-tax cost and the reduction in value. It is hardly a desirable situation. This is before considering the opportunity loss of the equity in the property—the earnings that could have been achieved if the equity was invested elsewhere.

This brings home an important consideration. To break even, the property will need to increase in value by the amount of the aggregate after-tax losses at the time of sale plus the costs of acquisition and costs of disposal (that is, the legal costs, stamp duty and real estate selling commission).

The success of a negative-gearing strategy is clearly dependent on the cash shortfall being exceeded by capital growth. This highlights the need for investment decisions to be made on the basis of tax savings. Negative gearing is a bonus, not the reason to invest. The decision should stack up on normal investment criteria. If it doesn't, an alternative should be sought.

That being said, historically real estate has outgrown inflation. But this does not mean that an increase in value is guaranteed. Nevertheless, I repeat what I said earlier; that is, I believe income-producing residential real estate has a place in any investment portfolio.

Austin Donnelly, in *Realistic Real Estate Investing*, displayed a chart showing movements in real estate property prices adjusted for inflation over the period 1960 to 1995. It was clear from the chart, and as interpreted by Mr Donnelly, that:

- Two periods, between 1969 and 1974, and 1985 and 1988, produced real gains of around 50 per cent.

- The five-year period after 1974 resulted in a decline of about 20 per cent.

- The period between 1988 and 1995 recorded a decline of around 10 per cent.

- There was no 'sustained net gain' between 1974 and 1986.

The period of 12 years between 1974 and 1986 was a long time to rent a loss.

Austin's call for caution should not go unheeded. Earlier in *Realistic Real Estate Investing*, he said:

> Since the end of the boom at about the end of 1988, housing prices have shown an almost negligible increase in nominal terms of less than 1 per cent per annum compound and a decline in real terms of about 1 per cent per annum compound.

A sobering thought. We all know that the market boomed again—perhaps history really does repeat?

Non-cash deductions

A key factor to consider is the effect of the non-cash deductions, which can increase the loss. These include borrowing costs, depreciation and the construction cost write-off. The example in appendix B shows depreciation of $928 and a construction cost write-off of $1750. These figures are used in the sample calculations that follow in table 12.2.

Table 12.2: sample calculation showing the effect of non-cash deductions

Net loss		$4715
less **non-cash items**		
Borrowing costs	$220	
Depreciation	$928	
Construction cost write-off	$1750	
	$2898	$2898
		$1817
Tax benefit @ 46.5%		$2192
Net cash surplus		**$375**

In this example, a tax loss of $1817 produced a net cash surplus of $375. This highlights how the success of a negative-gearing strategy is materially affected by the amount of the non-cash deductions.

When considering a property investment proposal, I use a spreadsheet to perform an analysis. An example follows in table 12.3 overleaf.

Table 12.3: property analysis Beenleigh proposed purchase 1 July 2008

Property cost	299 000	Construction cost	150 000
		Capital growth	5%
Depreciable items	10 000	Inflation rate	3%
		Interest rate	9.30%
Contract price	309 000	Occupancy rate	95%
		Property expenses	30%
		Building write-off	
Purchase costs	10 600	rate	2.50%
	319 600	**Depreciation rate**	
		Marginal tax rate	46.50%
Loan	300 000	Weekly rent	$160
		Borrowing costs	2 800
Equity	19 600	Period of loan	20 years

	2009	**2010**	**2011**	**2012**	**2013**
Cash flow analysis					
Gross rent	12 350	12 720	13 101	13 494	13 898
Cash deductions					
Loan interest	27 673	27 147	26 571	25 938	25 244
Property expenses	3 705	3 816	3 930	4 047	4 168
	31 378	30 963	30 501	29 985	29 412
Pre-tax cash flow	–19 028	–18 243	–17 400	–16 491	–15 514
Non–cash flow deductions					
Depreciation	1 500	1 275	1 083	921	783
Building cost write-offs	3 750	3 750	3 750	3 750	3 750
Borrowing costs	560	560	560	560	560
	5 810	5 585	5 393	5 231	5 093
Total deductions	37 188	36 548	35 894	35 216	34 505
Net income	–24 838	–23 828	–22 793	–21 722	–20 607

	2009	2010	2011	2012	2013
Tax credit	11549	11080	10598	10100	9582
After-tax cash flow before principal repayment	-7479	-7163	-6802	-6391	-5932
Property value	313950	329647	346129	363435	381606
Equity before loan repayment	14950	15697	16482	17306	18171
Principal repayment	5145	5940	6517	7150	7844
Equity	**20095**	**21637**	**22999**	**24456**	**26015**

In this example, the property was in Beenleigh, a town between Brisbane and the Gold Coast. The contract price was $309000. The builder provided a schedule that showed $10000 as the cost of the depreciable items, and $150000 as the construction cost for the building cost write-off. Legal costs and stamp duty amounted to $10600 and borrowing costs totalled $2800, on a principal and interest loan of $300000 at an interest rate of 9.3 per cent, with a term of 20 years. For the analysis I assumed a capital growth rate of 3 per cent per annum, inflation rate of 3 per cent, an occupancy rate of 95 per cent and property expenses of 30 per cent. The rental was $160 per week and the client was on the highest marginal tax rate.

The analysis disclosed that, if the assumptions proved to be correct, at the end of the fifth year my client's equity in the property would have grown from $20095 to $26015, an increase of around 129 per cent over the five years. (Note: the growth in property value has been based on the contract price of $309000, not the total cost of $319600. There is a valid argument that the figure of $299000 should be used as the basis for the growth, as the depreciable items will lose rather than gain value.) This illustrates the power of negative gearing. In each of the five years there was a positive after-tax cash flow, before accounting for the principal component of the loan repayment. The principal repayment can be looked at as compulsory saving.

You should perform this exercise with any proposed investment property. Change the variables to look at best and worst case alternatives. This way, an informed decision can be made.

The spreadsheet also showed the after-tax cash flow (before the principal repayment component) on the other marginal tax rates. See table 12.4 below.

Table 12.4: after-tax cash flow on the other marginal tax rates

Marginal tax rate %	2008	2009	2010	2011	2012
16.5	−14930	−14312	−13640	−12907	−12114
31.5	−11205	−10738	−10221	−9649	−9023
43.5	−8721	−8355	−7941	−7477	−6963

Negative gearing may well be an appropriate strategy, but do your sums first.

Chapter 13

Positive gearing

In an article I read recently, a real estate author was quoted as saying, 'Negative gearing is about borrowing money to lose money, while positive gearing is about borrowing money to make money'.

While I don't fully agree with that statement, the author is partly right. Without a corresponding increase in property value, the negatively geared investor is destroying—not creating—wealth. The reality, however, is that over a long period of time the capital gains from property normally far exceed the net loss incurred after taxation.

The article started with the line 'Most people lose money on property'. It quoted figures from the Australian Bureau of Statistics showing that:

• less than 30 per cent of property investors made a profit in 1995–96

- 11 per cent broke even
- 36 per cent made a loss
- the other 23 per cent did not know.

What the article failed to say was that there are two parts to a return on investment: the first is the income return; the second is the growth in the asset's value. The article did not account for this second element of rental property investment.

History has shown us that property prices grow over a long period of time. Property investment is a long-term venture and any analysis should be undertaken with that in mind. Investors must make their own minds up about the merits of negative gearing compared to positive gearing. They should do their sums and try not to be diverted by the part-truths or falsehoods such as those in the article discussed above.

A positively geared property is one where the property makes a profit after accounting for all costs, including interest, as in table 13.1. If such a property is in tax loss after deducting non–cash flow items such as decline in value, borrowing costs and the construction cost write-off, it is said to have a positive cash flow, as in table 13.2. A property with no borrowings has no gearing and would simply be described as being income-positive or income-negative.

Table 13.1: example of a positively geared property

Positively geared property		
Rent		$15 000
Expenses		
General	$6 000	
Interest	$2 000	
Capital allowance	$3 000	$12 000
Net income		**$2 000**

Table 13.2: example of a positive cash flow property

Positive cash flow property		
Rent		$15000
Expenses		
General	$6000	
Interest	$7000	
		$2000
Capital allowance		$3000
Net income		**$1000**

A net loss from rental investments reduces a taxpayer's assessable income. A net gain increases it.

Because of this, an investor may decide to have income-positive or positively geared (those properties with net incomes) asset owned by a family trust. This will provide some asset protection while allowing the income to be distributed in order to realise the best tax advantage. It will also enable a tax-beneficial distribution of capital gains when the time comes to sell the property.

The benefits of gearing

• You can invest more than you may have been able to.

• Your net percentage gains will be higher in a rising market.

The risks of gearing

• Your net percentage losses will be higher in a falling market.

• Rising interest rates may result in an inability to service a loan.

Chapter 14

Repairs and maintenance

With regards to taxation, a repair is an expense incurred in restoring an income-producing asset to the condition it was in when it first produced income. It is work performed to remedy a defect, damage or deterioration without changing an asset's character. That is, a repair remedies wear and tear.

In a letter to taxpayers dated 24 June 1997, the Commissioner of Taxation noted the following two areas of concern relating to repairs and maintenance:

1 initial repairs at the time of purchase

2 repairs versus improvements.

In my experience, many clients have difficulty understanding the distinction between a repair and an improvement. Occasionally, I suspect, they do not want to know the difference. However, reality bites and, like it or not, people must accept that a repair is an allowable deduction while an improvement is not. They must also accept that it is most unlikely that expenditure incurred in repairing problems existing at the time of purchase are anything other than an improvement.

Initial repairs at time of purchase

It may be obvious at the time of purchase of a property that work needs to be done to enable it to be rented. Walls may need to be painted, guttering replaced, holes in walls repaired, palings replaced on fences, among a host of things. Attending to these needs would result in expenditure that is capital in nature and not deductible. Clearly, they are improvements.

A reasonable person would conclude that an allowance would have been made, in coming to an agreement on the purchase price, for the items that need to be attended to. The subsequent expenditure would be part of the cost of purchase and this would be so even if a purchaser was unaware of the need for repair at the time of acquisition. There was a legal case where a claim for rewiring and replastering of a house was disallowed, despite the owner not being aware of the faults at purchase.

Repairs to former residence

It is possible that repair work may be required on a rental property that was formerly the owner's private residence. Some of the damage may be attributable to the period before the property was rented. However, a claim may still be available; providing the property is a rental at the time the expenditure is incurred. This is confirmed by TR 97/23 Income tax: deductions for repairs.

Clause 77 of that ruling reads:

> A deduction is allowable under section 25-10 if, when the repair expenditure is incurred in a year of income, the property is held, etc., by a taxpayer for income purposes:
>
> a   even though the property has previously been held, etc., by the taxpayer for non-income purposes; and
>
> b   even though some or all of the defects, damage or deterioration arise from, or are attributable to, the taxpayer's holding, etc., of the property before its holding, etc., for income purposes; and
>
> c   provided that the repair expenditure is not capital expenditure.

Repairs versus improvements

In his letter, the Commissioner said, 'You cannot claim a deduction for the costs of any alterations, additions or improvements, as they are a capital expense'.

Whether there has been an improvement rather than a repair will depend on the individual circumstances. There are numerous cases that can be reviewed to assist in determining whether there has been an improvement rather than a repair. For example, the courts have found that an underground drainage system that replaced a septic system was an improvement. Other instances include a concrete floor replacing a wooden floor, rectification of a pre-existing drainage fault, replacing an electrical system, a leaky roof being replaced with a cheaper sheet metal roof, a copper water service replacing galvanised water pipes and the replacement of a kitchen in a home unit. These were all found to be improvements.

Australian publishers CCH, in their *Australian Income Tax Guide*, reason that work done is 'more likely to be an improvement if' it:

*   results in less 'likelihood of future repairs'

*   increases the life of an asset

*   improves the asset's efficiency

*   is 'more expensive than using original materials'.

The guide claims work done is 'less likely to be an improvement if':

*   the result has 'disadvantages as well as advantages, for example, a longer wearing floor may be harder to walk on'.

*   the materials used are cheaper than the original materials.

Some examples where work was found not to be an improvement include:

*   the replacement of venetian blinds by cheaper casement windows

*   part-steel and part-timber uprights replacing timber uprights

*   foam insulation replacing timber and sawdust insulation

*   a concrete floor that was hard to walk on and not moisture-proof replacing a wooden basement floor.

It would be sensible, at the time the work is done, to obtain a letter from the tradesperson effecting the repair, verifying the work was to repair damage and not to simply make an improvement. It should be noted that the Tax Office accepts the work can still be a repair despite minor or incidental improvement that results from using new materials or technology.

Repair work can be carried out at the same time as an improvement, but it is necessary to separate the cost of the repair work from the improvement to obtain the deduction. If that cannot be done, the whole of the work would be regarded as being an improvement.

Repairs and the sale of a rental property

Repairs are sometimes required after a property ceases to earn income. A Taxation Board of Review case (12 TBRD, Case M2) disallowed a deduction for repairs carried out after a tenant had vacated the property, because it 'was then not held for the purpose of producing income, but for the purpose of realisation by sale'. However, the Commissioner will allow repairs after a property is no longer used to produce assessable income providing:

*   the repairs related to the time when the property was rented
*   the property was rented in the year in which the repairs were carried out.

I believe that these conditions are fair and reasonable. After all, costs to repair damage or wear and tear, which occurred while a property was rented, are clearly a cost of the rental and not of capital.

Care should be taken to ensure that the repair work meets the commissioner's conditions. This is based on the IT 180 ruling, which relates to a provision of the 1936 Act. Despite this, paragraph 74 of TR 97/23 (which follows) suggests that the claim may now be allowed.

> There may be occasions, however, where section 8-1 allows a deduction for repair expenditure that would otherwise not be deductible under section 25-10. Section 8-1 might allow a deduction, for example, after a taxpayer ceases to hold, etc., property for income

purposes even though section 25-10 would not allow a deduction (see *Placer Pacific Management Pty Limited v FC of T 95* ATC 4459; [1995] 31 ATR 253).

Complete replacement of an asset

It is well established that the replacement of an asset is a capital improvement and not a repair. For example, the replacement of a stove is capital expenditure. In this instance, however, the stove would be depreciable. Replacement of the elements on the stove that have ceased to function is a repair.

Common sense should prevail when making a claim for repairs. Taxpayers Australia, in their *2001 Tax Summary*, give an example that 'Some items last longer than others. Water pipes or guttering corroding within, say, five years may mean they probably needed replacing when purchased'.

Is it a repair for tax purposes?

Positive answers to the following questions may suggest that the required work constitutes a repair.

1   Does the repair restore the property to its original condition?

2   Is the property damaged?

3   Is the whole item renewed by replacing parts of the property progressively over time?

4   Does the expenditure involve the replacement of permanent fixtures?

5   Does the work remedy defects that occurred after the property was purchased?

6   Does the repair remedy defects arising before the property was rented but fixed while the property was rented?

7   Did the costs incurred after the property was sold or no longer rented relate to damage incurred while the property was rented?

Negative answers to the questions below may suggest (but not necessarily confirm) that the work in question is an improvement or capital expenditure.

1   Is the expenditure an initial repair?

2   Is the work undertaken with the sole purpose of preventing possible future damage?

3   Does the work increase the property's value?

4   Does the work change the character of the asset?

5   Is the asset replaced in its entirety?

6   Is the expenditure required to comply with a government regulation or order?

Chapter 15

A letter to an agent

The following is an example of how one needs to take care in selecting rental managers. What follows occurred. It is not fiction and it is not an isolated case, although the degree of negligence may not be the norm. A copy of this letter is in my client's file in my office.

---

16 July 2007
The Property Manager
XYZ Realty
XYZ Road
Anytown Qld

Dear Sir/Madam,

Re: 813 Anytown Drive, Anytown

I have been asked to write you this report in regard to problems associated with the former tenancy of

---

813 Anytown Drive. I do so despite not having received an inspection checklist or end-of-tenancy report from your office. The lease ended on the 7 July and tenant vacated the property on 4 July. I was not notified of the state of the unit on the tenant's exit.

Several items of disrepair, some of which are significant, had to be pointed out to your employees.

Defects have been overlooked

I had to point out major defects to your employees which had gone unnoticed. These included:

- An unsatisfactory cleaning job. The insides of wardrobes still require cleaning.

- Damaged screens on windows.

- Bird droppings covering the fence and garage.

- Weeds having overtaken the yard.

Animal-related damage

It was made clear to your agency that no pets were to be allowed in the unit. Your office was notified several times that there was a dog in the unit and no action was taken.

Your employee, June, informed me she had inspected the property and had found no evidence of a dog living there. This was despite me advising her that I saw the former tenant take a dog inside. I accepted that this may have been a one-off occasion. The evidence proves this was not the case.

It is clear no inspection was made after obtaining an admission that the former tenant had been looking after a dog for two weeks. If there had been an inspection, the damage would have been noticed and would not be as significant as it is.

Carpet damage

June, a property manager under your employ claims that as the carpet is over ten years old a court would say the carpet is beyond its economic life. That argument is based on a case where worn carpet had been removed by a tenant.

The carpet in the unit was in excellent condition before the unit was tenanted. It had a life well in excess of five years. Permanent stains, tears and advice from a floor technician that smells would remain despite cleaning mean that I have to replace it. Aside from the damage there are no worn areas. I therefore have a right to reimbursement for the cost of replacement.

Prior to my purchase, the unit was not rented twelve months a year. This means it was not subject to normal usage. It is unjust that I should incur this cost, which is a result of willful damage by the former tenant by keeping a dog locked up inside, allowing it to drop faeces and urinate and scratch out and destroy portions of the carpet. Some consideration has to be taken in that the carpet, despite its original condition at the commencement of the tenancy, was not new. I believe I am entitled to at least half the cost of replacement of a quality carpet throughout the premises.

Defect summary

A defect summary follows. This is not complete and I reserve the right to make claim to remedy any further defect noted after the time of this letter, which was the result of the tenancy. It is not my responsibility to supply this list. It should have been generated by your office as part of the management of the property.

Throughout

- Unit keys, swipes and security sticks should have been given to me on vacation of the unit. (I am still waiting for the swipes and stick.)

- I was told that cleaners were employed for two days. The job done by the cleaners was unsatisfactory.

Garage

- Acid build-up, filth and marks on the garage floor need to be cleaned with a gurney to remove the acid markings and sweeping to remove the dirt.

- The garage door's manual operation handle was broken off and left lying on the garage floor. This is not normal wear and tear and it is the responsibility of the former tenant to have this fixed.

Yard

- The front yard was landscaped prior to the unit being tenanted. Mondo grass needs to be replaced between concrete slabs. This has been accepted as requiring rectification.

- Garbage needs to be removed from the front yard.

- Garage walls and fence need to be cleaned of bird droppings.

Main bedroom

- There are dog and mouse faeces and urine stains on the doonas, pillows and bed coverings. As I will not be letting a furnished unit in future, I now require payment for the cost of replacement, rather than replacement.

- The double-screen sliding door is jammed and its screen is torn.

Bedroom 2

- Dog urine stains throughout.

- Screen torn multiple times by dog paws.

- Hole in plaster from when the bed-head was ripped from the wall.

Bedroom 3

- Marks on walls require removal.

- A vertical blind needs to be repaired.

- Window screen and screen frame needs to be replaced.

Wardrobes, linen cupboard and storage areas

- These are all filthy and need to be cleaned.

Main living and dining area

- Urine stains are evident even after carpet cleaning.

- Lounge room and dining room sliding doors need to be fixed.

- Screen door on double sliding door at far end of dining area has been torn as a result of forced entry.

- The carpet at the base of the column has been torn away.

Kitchen

- Repairs to the plaster work on the ceiling are required as a result of the former tenant's failure to notify you of a leak in bathroom in a timely manner.

- Kitchen floor has not been cleaned and dust needs to be removed from vents in oven.

- The phone was taken from the kitchen wall. This needs to be replaced.

Staircase

- There are marks on walls along the length of the staircase.

- A red ink stain on the upper level of the staircase needs to be removed.

Alcove area

- Dog urine and faeces stains, and a blue ink stain still remain evident on carpet after cleaning.

- Tear in carpet in join between alcove and main bedroom.

Bathroom

- I am unhappy with the repairs made to the tiles behind the bathroom door. These were attended to at my cost by your tiler during the rental. I have no problem with the fact that the tiles could not be matched exactly, but they have not been laid flat, resulting in damage to kitchen ceiling. This is unacceptable and I request that you attend to rectification at the tiler's cost. It seems that neither you, nor your employees have inspected that repair work.

The above defects are not all-encompassing. Others are known to your employees. Some of these issues have been attended to.

Inspection reports and pest control receipt

In view of the above, I request copies of inspection checklists and a receipt to prove pest control has been attended to since the tenant's departure.

Reimbursement of rent

I have had to pay rent for an extra week because of problems caused by the former tenant. This is the result of your failure to manage the property and remedy defects. I therefore seek compensation of $320 for the extra expense incurred.

Whether that comes from the former tenant, insurance or the agent is of no concern to me. Should it not come from the former tenant or insurance, redress will be sought from your office.

I received no communication stating that the tenant had not signed a new lease and only discovered this when I queried your office some time after the lease had expired.

I have been told the former tenant's parents have six or so properties with your agency. I feel the former tenant's interests were being looked after, rather than my own and believe this to be the reason.

I allege you have been derelict in your duties. I have received only one inspection report during the concluded tenancy. The state of the unit upon vacation suggests that this very broad and incomplete note (which is all it was) was not factual.

In the absence of an exit report, I can only conclude that matters I discovered would be attended to and those I didn't would be left. I have discovered that another former landlord you represented had similar problems.

I have been lied to by your representative, June. I was made aware at the start of the lease that a young man was going to be living there but that the agent would be supervising closely.

My partner was told by June after I learned of the mess that this was not the case; that a young couple had signed the lease and was living there. This was a blatant untruth to try and deflect responsibility from the agent.

I have received legal advice that the agent has been negligent and is liable for any economic loss I have suffered as a result of the state in which the unit was left. Nothing in this report is to be taken as removing any rights I may have for any claim against your office for damages in compensation for your mismanagement of the unit.

Yours faithfully,

A Disgruntled Landlord

The result

Inspection checklists were not produced. Neither was the receipt to prove pest control had been attended. It is doubtful that inspections were made and the pest control was not undertaken.

The agent took steps to recover damages from the former tenant's parents, who were his guarantors. These were spent on attending to the repairs and replacing the carpet. No compensation was offered for lost rent but my client accepted that he was lucky to get as much as he had and that the costs of pursuing this further outweighed any likely additional compensation.

The tax effect

Costs incurred in rectifying the damage as the result of the rental were deductible to the extent that they restored the unit to the condition it was in when it first produced income.

The reimbursement for those costs was assessable income. The cost of replacing the carpet was not an outright deduction but was depreciable.

Real estate agents: an opinion

As a result of personal experience and what I have been told by many clients, my view in respect to rental agents' value has diminished to the extent that if asked as to whether one should be engaged, my answer would be 'probably not'. They are often overpaid rent collectors. There are some who do a good job but it is difficult to find them. Unfortunately, the job the good rental agents do is tarnished by the poor performance of others. Part of the problem is that the agents have too many properties to manage. As a result, happenings such as the one outlined in this chapter occur.

Chapter 16

Other tax matters

Tax office common error circular

In 2005 the Tax Office issued a circular stating it had identified common mistakes made by taxpayers declaring rental income and claiming deductions. It listed these as follows:

- Incorrectly claiming 'the cost of the land as a capital works deduction; that is, as part of the cost of constructing or renovating the rental property'.

- Incorrectly claiming 'the cost of improvements such as remodelling bathrooms or kitchens or adding a deck or pergola as repairs. These are capital improvements and should be claimed as capital works deductions'.

- Overstating 'claims for deductions on the interest on the loan taken out to purchase, renovate or maintain the property. A loan may be taken out for both income-producing and private purposes, such as to purchase motor vehicles or other goods or services. The interest on this private portion of the loan is not deductible and should not be claimed'.

- Incorrectly claiming 'the full cost of an inspection visit when it is combined with another private purpose, such as a holiday. In such cases, you can only claim that portion of the travel costs that relate directly to the property inspection'.

- Claiming 'deductions for properties [that] are not genuinely available for rent'.

- Incorrectly 'claiming deductions when properties are only available for rent for part of the year. If a holiday home or unit is used by you or your friends or your relatives free of charge for part of the year, you are not entitled to a deduction for costs incurred during those periods'.

- Claiming 'deductions for items incorrectly classified as depreciating assets. We have produced a comprehensive list of more than 230 residential property items identifying whether they are depreciating assets eligible for a decline in value deduction, or as assets eligible for a capital works deduction'.

- 'If you financed the purchase of your rental property using a split loan facility, you cannot claim a deduction for the extra capitalised interest expense imposed under that facility'.

Commercial rents

Chris is a client of mine who owns a unit at Surfers Paradise. His daughter has a job on the Gold Coast, so Chris decided she could stay in the unit rather than commute from Brisbane each day. Wanting to do the right thing, he charged her $50 per week rent. A commercial rent for that unit on permanent letting would be $220 per week.

Chris was an unhappy person after leaving my office. The property was no longer let on a commercial basis and the effect was that the income was assessable, but the expenses were only deductible to the extent of the rent received. He could not afford to continue to forego the loss incurred, so his daughter found someone to share the unit with her and now pays a commercial rent, and the status has been restored.

Costs after property rental has ceased

Tim and Diane decided that they were going to sell their rental property. The tenants had left, it was proving difficult to re-let and they felt their money was better placed elsewhere. The property had been in good condition when it was first let. But a number of repairs were needed after the tenants vacated. The good news for my clients was that as the premises produced income in the year the expenditure was incurred, and as the need for the repairs could be related to the time the property was rented, the repairs were deductible.

Splitting the interest expense

Bill and Jane came to see me for the first time. They had been doing their returns themselves but realised they may not have been claiming their full entitlement. Bill had a taxable income of $90 000 and Jane $20 000. This was before offsetting the loss from their rental property.

On reviewing the previous years' returns I noticed that Bill was claiming a deduction for interest whereas Jane was not. My new clients had brought the loan documentation with them and it clearly showed that the loan was in joint names and that the property was jointly owned. The agent's statements were in joint names, as was the bank account into which the rental payments were deposited. Bill argued that as his funds were being used to make the repayments the interest was deductible to him alone. Not so. Although the interest deduction was of more value to Bill than Jane, it had to be apportioned equally. He reluctantly accepted that amended returns had to be prepared for prior years, accepting the penalties would be significantly less as a result of his voluntary disclosure.

Although there was an initial tax disadvantage, it does not change my opinion that, generally, rental property ownership should be in joint names. Eventually the property should become income-positive, and the losses would more than be made up for in the years to come.

What to do if asset values aren't specified

Terry and Robyn came in with the details of their newly acquired rental property. Their record keeping was immaculate. However, I noted the blank looks when I asked for a statement of assets acquired with the property. They said the previous owner had rented the property but was reluctant to disclose his depreciation details.

I advised that they engage the services of a quantity surveyor to calculate the values. This is a better alternative than attempting to establish realistic values themselves. The quantity surveyor included items that may have otherwise been missed and, as he was at arms-length, provided a base on which the taxpayers could be confident of their claim. Rather this than running the risk of getting it wrong.

Family home in the trust

Some accountants advise purchasing the family home in a trust that operates the family business. Borrowings are arranged in the trust and the home rented by the family members at a commercial rate. The trust then lodges a return declaring the rental as income and claiming the allowable outgoings as deductions. The losses arising from the rental are offset against other trust income. If the home had been purchased by the family, the outgoings would not have been deductible. In 1985 the Taxation Board of Review overturned the Tax Office view that the rent is not assessable income to the trust and that the losses and outgoings are not deductible.

I am not convinced of the soundness of these arrangements. It is long-established business practice that personal capital assets should not be held by trading entities so as not to expose them to business risk. This can be avoided by setting up a second trust to own the property. Income is then distributed to this trust from the trading trust to absorb the loss from the rental and not expose the rental property to the business risk inherent in the trading trust.

The family home is exempt from capital gains tax. That exemption does not apply if the family home is owned by a trust. I always try to take a long-term view—the short-term gain of negative gearing losses may well be more than offset by a potential CGT liability on sale of the home in the future.

Interest payments prior to income

Delays in the construction of a rental property may result in interest being incurred before rental is received. The High Court, in *Steele v DFC* of T 99 ATC, determined that interest paid in relation to the purchase or construction of an asset that is to be used to produce income may be claimed before income is earned. This represents a return to the status that existed before the Federal Court found differently in that case. The rejection of the Federal Court's finding has resulted in the Commissioner issuing TR 2000/17. This draft ruling reflects the Commissioner's opinion that interest incurred in a period prior to derivation of assessable income will be deductible providing:

- the interest is not incurred 'too soon', is not preliminary to the income earning activities and is not a prelude to those activities

- the interest is not private or domestic

- the period of interest outgoings prior to the derivation of relevant assessable income is not so long, taking into account the kind of income-earning activities involved, that the necessary connection between outgoings and assessable income is lost

- the interest is incurred with one end in view: the gaining or producing of assessable income

- continuing efforts are undertaken in pursuit of that end.

Former residence rented then sold

Gary and Ros purchased their home in 1987. It was their first home, a neat and tidy three-bedroom chamfer-board house at Mt Gravatt (a suburb on Brisbane's southside). The business that the couple ran went from strength to strength and, wanting to reap the benefits of their increased prosperity, they decided to upgrade. However, rather than selling, they decided to keep the Mt Gravatt property as a rental.

Three years ago, a chance arose to expand their business, but the growth could only be financed by sale of the rental property.

Having purchased well, they were looking at a capital gain of over $40 000 after indexation. They came to me concerned as to their possible tax liability. The news was good. The property had only been rented for three years. It was originally their principal place of residence and they were able to make an election that meant it was exempt from CGT. That exemption carried through for the period that it was owned as a rental property. This is because they were away from the home for less than six years.

You can elect to retain the principal residence exemption for your home if it is used to produce rental income providing you are not absent from it for more than six years. You do not need to reoccupy the home before its sale to keep the benefit.

You must make the election, in writing, no later than the date the return for the income year in which the property is sold is lodged. However, the Tax Office has the power to extend this time.

It is important to note that you can only have one sole or principal residence. In Gary and Ros's case, their new home would only be their principal residence from the date of sale of the other home.

Chapter 17

Losses on rental property

It is time to consider the arithmetic of the tax effect of a loss from a rental property. For this I have assumed a net loss of $3000.

Table 17.1 shows the tax rates for Australian residents, including the 1.5 per cent Medicare levy, for the 2007–08 year at the time of writing (March 2008).

Table 17.1: tax rates for 2007–08

Taxable income ($)	Marginal tax rate (%)
0–6000	Nil
6001–30000	16.5
30001–75000	31.5
75001–150000	41.5
150001+	46.5

I see little point in showing a table that excludes the Medicare levy. The levy is a reality and a tax. It is semantics to argue that the top marginal rate is 45 per cent on to which is added a 1.5 per cent Medicare levy. The rate is 46.5 per cent. Ask those who pay it.

There is an income threshold up to which no Medicare levy is applied, but it is ignored for the purpose of this exercise. For those who are interested, however, the following taxpayers are not required to pay this levy:

- single persons with taxable income less than $16740

- couples/sole parents with taxable income less than $28247 (with an additional threshold of $2594 for each dependent child and/or student).

There is a 1 per cent surcharge that applies to single taxpayers with a taxable income greater than $100000, or couples with a taxable income greater than $150000, who do not have private hospital cover. As this is a discretionary tax — that is, it can be avoided by taking out private health insurance — it is also ignored for this exercise.

Table 17.2 shows the after-tax cost of a $3000 loss at the different marginal tax rates.

Table 17.2: after-tax cost of a $3000 loss

Marginal tax rate (%)	16.5	31.5	41.5	46.5
Net rental loss ($)	3000	3000	3000	3000
Tax reduction ($)	495	945	1245	1395
After-tax cost ($)	2505	2055	1755	1605

It is clear that the loss is much less costly for a taxpayer on the highest marginal rate. But the prime consideration is that the cost is still significant, and if the property is not increasing in value the landlord is $1605 worse off (on a marginal tax rate of 46.5 per cent) than if he or she did not own the property.

Splitting the loss

Table 17.3 shows that the costs, after splitting the income with a spouse who has no income, is $697 per year more than if the property was owned solely by the breadwinner on a marginal tax rate of 46.5 per cent. However, that does not mean the property should be in the name of the breadwinner. In the first instance, the spouse's share of the loss would be carried forward indefinitely and offset against future income. Second, if the property were sold in the future and a capital gain incurred, the tax on the gain may be significantly less if the income were split than if the property were in the hands of the breadwinner alone.

Table 17.3: costs after splitting income with a spouse with no income

Marginal tax rate (%)	16.5	31.5	41.5	46.5
Net rental loss ($)	1500	1500	1500	1500
Tax reduction ($)	248	473	623	698
After-tax cost ($)	1252	1027	877	802
After-tax cost to spouse ($)	1500	1500	1500	1500
Total after-tax cost ($)	**2752**	**2527**	**2377**	**2302**

Capital gains tax

Let's assume that the property is held for three years and sold at a net capital gain of $30000. Table 17.4 assumes that the spouse has no income.

Table 17.4: capital gains tax for spouse with no income

Marginal tax rate (%)	16.5	31.5	41.5	46.5
Capital gains tax ($)	4950	9450	12450	13950
Savings: joint names ($)	1125	2970	4875	5625

The spouse would pay tax of $1350 on his or her share of the gain.

At the highest marginal tax rate, $5625 would be saved in CGT by having the property in joint names. If we assume that the costs were similar in the three years, this is a net saving of $3531 after deducting the tax saving forgone for the loss in those years.

Spouse with income

Next we consider the situation where the spouse has income and the property is in joint names. The $3000 loss becomes a loss of $1500 each. Table 17.5 shows the after-tax cost.

This can be compared to the cost when the property is solely owned by one partner in table 17.6.

Table 17.5: $3000 loss after tax

Marginal tax rate	$
Both partners on 16.5%	2505
One partner on 16.5%; other on 31.5%	2280
One partner on 16.5%; other on 41.5%	2130
One partner on 16.5%; other on 46.5%	2055
Both partners on 31.5%	2055
One partner on 31.5%; other on 41.5%	1905
One partner on 31.5%; other on 46.5%	1830

Marginal tax rate	$
Both partners on 41.5%	1755
One partner on 41.5%; other on 46.5%	1680
Both partners on 46.5%	1605

Table 17.6: $3000 loss as sole or joint owner

Marginal tax rate	Sole owner ($)	Joint ($)	Cost ($)
Both partners on 16.5%	2505	2505	0
One partner on 16.5%; other on 31.5%	2505	2280	225
One partner on 16.5%; other on 41.5%	2505	2130	375
One partner on 16.5%; other on 46.5%	2505	2055	450
Both partners on 31.5%	2055	2055	0
One partner on 31.5%; other on 41.5%	2055	1905	150
One partner on 31.5%; other on 46.5%	2055	1830	225
Both partners on 41.5%	1755	1755	0
One partner on 41.5%; other on 46.5%	1755	1680	75
Both partners on 46.5%	1605	1605	0

Income positive

What if the property becomes income-positive and nets $4000 after expenses? Table 17.7 overleaf shows that with a marginal tax rate of 46.5 per cent, tax of $1860 is payable, leaving $2140 from $4000 net income after tax.

The situation changes if the property is in joint names, and one spouse has no other income (see table 17.8).

Table 17.7: income-positive property

Marginal tax rate (%)	16.5	31.5	41.5	46.5
Net rental income ($)	4000	4000	4000	4000
Tax payable ($)	660	1260	1660	1860
Net income after tax ($)	**3340**	**2740**	**2340**	**2140**

Table 17.8: income-positive property in joint names

Marginal tax rate (%)	16.5	31.5	41.5	46.5
Net rental income ($)	2000	2000	2000	2000
Tax payable ($)	330	630	830	930
Loss of spouse rebate ($)	430	430	430	430
Tax effect ($)	760	1060	1260	1360
Net income after tax ($)	1240	940	740	640
Spouse after-tax income ($)	2000	2000	2000	2000
Total after-tax income ($)	**3240**	**2940**	**2740**	**2640**

If the property is owned by the breadwinner, he or she will be $500 worse off per year on a marginal tax rate of 46.5 per cent under this scenario.

A long-term view

Table 17.9 shows the amortisation schedule is for a principal and interest loan with the following assumptions:

- borrowing: $120000

- interest rate: 6.7 per cent

- term: 20 years.

The figures in table 17.9 are used in the analysis that follows in table 17.10, which is an extension of the example set out in chapter 12. The calculations show that the property becomes tax income-positive in the seventeenth year. No allowance has been made for replacement of depreciable assets. In this example, the depreciation deduction expired in the seventh year. A tax rate of 46.5 per cent is assumed.

If a loan acceleration program was entered into, the property would become income-positive earlier.

Table 17.9: amortisation schedule for 20-year loan

Yr	Repayment ($)	Interest ($)	Principal ($)	Balance ($)
0				300 000
1	33 088	27 673	5 415	294 585
2	33 088	27 147	5 940	288 644
3	33 088	26 571	6 517	282 127
4	33 088	25 938	7 150	274 977
5	33 088	25 244	7 844	267 133
6	33 088	24 482	8 605	258 527
7	33 088	23 647	9 440	249 086
8	33 088	22 731	10 357	238 729
9	33 088	21 726	11 362	227 367
10	33 088	20 623	12 465	214 902
11	33 088	19 413	13 675	201 227
12	33 088	18 086	15 002	186 225
13	33 088	16 629	16 459	169 766
14	33 088	15 032	18 056	151 710
15	33 088	13 279	19 809	131 901
16	33 088	11 356	21 732	110 169
17	33 088	9 247	23 841	86 328
18	33 088	6 932	26 156	60 172
19	33 088	4 394	28 694	31 478
20	33 088	1 610	31 479	0

Table 17.10: cash-flow analysis of an amortised loan

	Year 1	Year 11	Year 15	Year 20	Year 25	Year 30
Cash flow analysis						
Gross rent	12 350	16 592	18 672	21 644	25 088	29 082
Cash deductions						
Loan interest	27 673	19 413	13 279	1 610	0	0
Property expenses	3 705	4 973	5 595	6 483	7 513	8 708
	31 378	24 386	18 874	8 093	7 513	8 708
Pre-tax cash-flow	−19 028	−7 794	−202	13 551	17 575	20 374
Non-cash flow deductions						
Decline in value	1 500	0	0	0	0	0
Building write off	3 750	3 750	3 750	3 750	3 750	3 750
Borrowing costs	560	0	0	0	0	0
	5 810	3 750	3 750	3 750	3 750	3 750
Total deductions	37 188	28 136	22 624	11 843	11 263	12 458
Net income	−24 838	−11 544	−3 952	9 801	13 825	16 624
Tax credit	**11 550**	**5 368**	**1 838**	**−4 557**	**−6 428**	**−7 730**
After tax cash flow						
Before principal repayment	**−7 478**	**−2 426**	**1 636**	**8 994**	**11 147**	**12 644**

The tax effect of joint ownership with a non-working spouse, ignoring other factors such as the effect of CGT (and the possible add-back of the construction cost write-back in that calculation, which affects properties purchased after 13 May 1997) is shown in table 17.11. The figures have not been calculated to allow for the effect of loss of any part of the dependent spouse rebate. In 2008 the dependent spouse rebate is $2100. The rebate reduces by $1 for every $4 of separate net income earned by the spouse over $282. This means that the rebate cuts out completely at a separate net income of $8681.

Table 17.11: tax effect of an amortised loan

Yr	Tax for-gone	Tax saved	Cumu-lative net	Yr	Tax for-gone	Tax saved	Cumu-lative net
1	5774		5774	16	381		54334
2	5540		11314	17		203	53496
3	5299		16613	18		838	51968
4	5050		21663	19		1528	49690
5	4791		26454	20		2278	46932
6	4235		30689	21		2758	44065
7	3970		34659	22		2867	41086
8	3685		38344	23		2979	37872
9	3378		41722	24		3095	34536
10	3045		44767	25		3214	31073
11	2684		47451	26		3336	27480
12	2295		50746	27		3463	23754
13	1873		51619	28		3593	19889
14	1415		53034	29		3726	19889
15	919		53953	30		3865	19889

Table 17.12: cash-flow analysis of joint ownership with a non-working spouse

	Year 1	Year 11	Year 15	Year 20	Year 25	Year 30
Cash flow analysis						
Gross rent	12350	16592	18672	21644	25088	29082
Cash deductions						
Loan interest	27673	19413	13279	1610	0	0
Property expenses	3705	4973	5595	6483	7513	8708
	31378	24386	18874	8093	7513	8708
Pre-tax cash-flow	−19028	−7794	−202	13551	17575	20374
Non-cash flow deductions						
Decline in value	1500	0	0	0	0	0
Building write-off	3750	3750	3750	3750	3750	3750
Borrowing costs	560	0	0	0	0	0
	5810	3750	3750	3750	3750	3750
Total deductions	37188	28136	22624	11843	11263	12458
Net income	−24838	−11544	−3952	9801	13825	16624
Tax credit	**5775**	**2684**	**919**	**−2278**	**−3214**	**−3865**
After-tax cash flow						
Before principal repayment	**−13253**	**−5110**	**717**	**11273**	**14361**	**16509**

It is evident that in table 17.12, the tax forgone is not recovered for some years. However, it is most likely that any cost in this respect will be recovered in capital gains tax when the property is sold.

These are examples only. The importance of the tax effect of the non-cash deductions cannot be emphasised enough. However, with the construction cost write-off now reducing the cost base of assets for properties acquired after 13 May 1997, the capital gains consequence of the tax write-back in the return of the higher income earner must be considered, as in table 17.13.

Table 17.13: tax effect of joint ownership with a non-working spouse

Yr	Tax for-gone	Tax saved	Cumu-lative net	Yr	Tax for-gone	Tax saved	Cumu-lative net
1	870		−870	16		611	−1286
2	794		−1664	17		694	−592
3	714		−2378	18		781	189
4	629		−3007	19		874	1063
5	540		−3547	20		973	2036
6	394		−3941	21		992	3028
7	295		−4236	22		1010	4038
8		41	−4195	23		1030	5068
9		144	−4051	24		1050	6118
10		201	−3850	25		1070	7188
11		259	−3591	26		1091	8279
12		322	−3269	27		1113	9329
13		381	−2888	28		1135	10527
14		459	−2429	29		1156	11683
15		532	−1897	30		1179	12862

Figure 17.1 below gives an indication as to the age of investors who purchased their first rental property in 1997. It is interesting to note that 70 per cent were under 44 years of age. This is significant when considering the number of potential years a rental property might be owned, and before dismissing the projection of the above figures for a period of 30 years.

Figure 17.1: rental investors by age when first became landlord (1993)

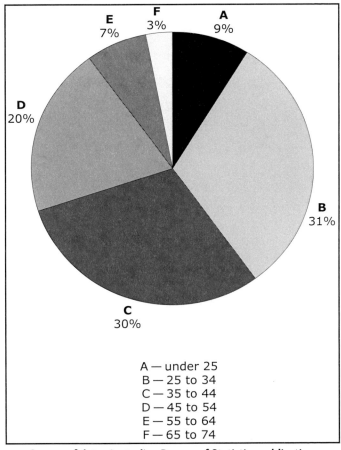

E 7%
F 3%
A 9%
D 20%
B 31%
C 30%

A — under 25
B — 25 to 34
C — 35 to 44
D — 45 to 54
E — 55 to 64
F — 65 to 74

Source of data: Australian Bureau of Statistics publication
Investors in Rental Dwellings Australia, July 1993

Chapter 18

Structures and ownership

Professional advice should be sought as to the most appropriate structure for owning income-producing property. Circumstances differ and what may be appropriate for one person may not be for another. However, the discussion below may, from a tax perspective, prove to be of some assistance in deciding who should own the property.

Sole ownership

In my experience, more rental properties in recent years have been purchased by the breadwinner than any other structure. The Australian Bureau of Statistics publication *Household Investors in Rental Dwellings Australia June 1997* states that 47.1 per cent of owners are individuals and 52.8 per cent purchased their rental property with a spouse or partner. This does not confirm my experience; and I suspect that this may not reflect the current situation. This is because advice is being given without regard to the long term, or to varying individual circumstances, and because of a belief that negatively geared assets should be held by the main income earner.

Although commonplace and simple, it does not necessarily follow that this advice is right. The income is derived by the individual, expenses are incurred by the individual and tax levied accordingly. There is no flexibility to split income or capital gains. Nor is there any asset protection in the event of financial problems. Any losses incurred are offset against the other income of the individual.

Joint ownership

The income is taxed in the proportion of ownership and, as with sole ownership, there is no asset protection. Losses are split in the proportion of the ownership.

Companies

Since September 1985 and the introduction of capital gains tax, companies have not been appropriate vehicles to hold investment properties. This has been the case even more so since the 1997 Budget, which included measures to restrict dividend streaming, thus removing the only flexibility provided by companies. Up until September 1999, CGT was subjected to only the non-inflationary component of the gain (that is, the real gain). Indexation has since been frozen and a CGT discount introduced. This discount does not apply to companies. Any benefit offered by indexation is lost when the gain is distributed to the shareholders. While on the surface asset protection is offered, in reality the property is at risk because of exposure to the ownership of the shares held in the company. Any losses earned are retained in the company for offset against other income earned by the company.

Family discretionary trusts

There is no doubt that the most flexible and often appropriate vehicle by which to own an investment property is a family discretionary trust. This is particularly so when there are no borrowings. Income and capital gains can be distributed to beneficiaries at the discretion of the trustee. Asset protection is provided because litigation against a beneficiary cannot affect any of the trust's assets. New beneficiaries can be added, increasing the income distribution flexibility, and the indexation factor is not lost if capital gains are distributed. The CGT discount applies to trusts. However, if a property is negatively geared, there would need to be other income earned by the trust to offset the loss. The losses cannot be distributed to the beneficiaries. This structure is therefore not appropriate, asset-protection considerations aside, for negatively geared investments when there is no other income to offset the loss.

Before deciding that a trust is the better structure, consideration must be given to the costs of establishment, the possibility that land tax may be incurred as a result of lower thresholds applicable to trusts than with individuals, and the costs of administration. These costs may well outweigh the benefits.

For some time, the Taxation Office and social welfare lobby groups have attempted to convince the government that trusts should be taxed in the same manner as companies. To date, they have been unsuccessful. With the enormous voting power of small business, and the popularity of trusts as a trading vehicle for small business, I doubt such a change will ever be made.

Your circumstances

When you seek advice as to the appropriate structure to use, the accountant will consider (among other things) the following:

- your age
- your family situation
- your income level
- your spouse's income
- the taxation effect of rental income and expenditure
- the non-cash deductions
- the cost of the structure (both initial and continuing)
- the cost of the investment and need for asset protection
- any land tax implications
- the level of gearing
- the type of loan
- your long-term goals
- the risks involved.

It will help if you provide him or her with these details in writing before your visit.

Chapter 19

Hybrid trusts

Justin is a university lecturer, with a non-working wife and two children. His income is $70 000. He has a share portfolio in his wife's name and no other income. He phoned me and announced he was about to sign a contract on an investment property. He was using the equity in his home as security and only had a small deposit. He told me that, on the advice from someone in the commerce faculty, he had set up a trust and wanted to use the trust to own the property. I asked him why. His answer was that he wanted asset protection. I asked what risks he was protecting himself from. He wasn't in business, it was unlikely that he was going to be sued as a result of his occupation and he had no equity in the property to protect. He answered that he was concerned that someone may damage themselves in the property and that he may be exposed to liability. I told him that he had been listening to too much theory and that he should have third party indemnity insurance to cover the unlikely event that that may happen.

He agreed but then said he wanted the flexibility to distribute income to his spouse and children, but the property was going to be negatively geared and he would want the loss to be offset against his income. I explained that losses cannot be distributed; that they remain within the trust and are then offset against future income the trust may earn. Justin explained that his trust is a hybrid trust. His colleague had explained that he should borrow to buy those units and claim the interest as a deduction. Then, when the trust earns money, he can distribute the income to his wife and children.

Justin had attended a seminar where he had been told that the trust had this flexibility and that not many accountants know about these things. Each year two or three clients will go walkabout because they hear things like this and don't check. It's frustrating, because these people act on what they want to believe rather than reality.

The speakers at the seminar had mentioned tax rulings and tax law and were of the opinion that the rulings were wrong, and they were going to test them. I asked Justin if he was interested in being a test case. When he said that he wasn't, I explained that there are two private binding rulings. They are based on solid case law and that my opinion is that the rulings are correct. I then directed him to the ATO website to look them up.

Justin ended up buying the property in joint names with his wife. He understood the advantages and disadvantages of doing this and took pleasure in educating his colleague from the commerce department.

What is a hybrid trust?

A hybrid trust is a trust that combines the features of a unit and a discretionary trust.

A unit trust entitles unitholders to a fixed entitlement to the capital and income of the trust in accordance with their unitholding. A discretionary trust allows distribution of the capital and income of the trust to the beneficiaries at the discretion of the trustee.

The strategy

Let's assume Justin had proceeded with the advice he was given by his colleague and that was touted at the investment property seminar. First off he would, as he had already done when he contacted me, set up his hybrid trust. Preferably this would have been done with a corporate trustee. His trust was set up with his family members automatically included with a beneficial interest in both the capital and the income of the trust.

His next step would be to borrow funds to enable him to subscribe for units in the hybrid trust. As Justin would have had no equity in the units, they would have been totally geared.

The trustee would then use the money received for the units to purchase a rental property.

Most likely the lender would have taken a mortgage over the property as security for Justin's loan.

The hybrid trust would earn income from the rental of the house and would pay the rental expenses.

Justin would be the sole unitholder. Because of this he would be entitled to all of the income. He would declare this in his income tax return and claim the interest incurred in financing the units.

The deed would normally provide that distributions to the beneficiaries (his family members) could normally only be made when Justin ceases to be a unitholder and there were no other unitholders.

When the time comes that the rent exceeds the interest on the loan Justin will redeem his units at the original issue price. This means that he would not realise a capital gain. The income would then be distributed to his family members at the discretion of the trustee so as to minimise the tax paid on that income.

At a later date, if the property were sold, the capital gain would also be distributed among the beneficiaries for best tax benefit.

The problem

A taxpayer may claim interest as a tax deduction providing it is incurred in gaining or producing assessable income and is not of a capital, private or domestic nature. This means that the use to which the money has been put needs to be considered. There does not need to be an immediate earning of income, but there needs to be an expectation that this will occur. That is, that eventually, income would exceed the expenditure. The courts have determined that a deduction is available as long as there is an expectation that this will happen and that the intention is that the investment will run its normal course.

When a taxpayer enters into a rental property negative gearing arrangement though an investment in a negative gearing hybrid trust, a difficulty arises. The nature of the arrangement is such that the intention is that the investment not run its full course. The intention is that the units be redeemed before the return to the unitholder becomes positively geared.

The result would be that the Tax Office would limit the claim for interest to the level of the distribution from the hybrid trust. That is unless the unitholder could establish that it was his or her intention that the arrangement become positively geared. In my opinion, it is most unlikely, given the nature of the hybrid trust, the unitholder could be successful in proving this.

Tax Office Rulings

Private Binding Ruling 66594

Can a deduction be claimed for interest paid on a loan used to invest in a hybrid unit trust where there is income received in the form of a distribution from the hybrid trust?

No.

Private Binding Ruling 65710

1 Is interest payable by the taxpayer on a bank loan for the acquisition of income units in the trust deductible under section 8-1 of the ITAA 1997?

   No.

2 Can interest payable by the taxpayer on a bank loan for the acquisition of income units in the trust be deducted under section 8-1 of the ITAA 1997 against the taxpayer's assessable income in the event of a negative return?

   No.

Private Binding Ruling 66298

1 Can you claim a full deduction for interest payable on your bank loan under section 8-1 of the ITAA 1997 for the acquisition of income units in a hybrid trust?

   No.

2 Can you claim a full deduction for annual interest payable on your bank loan under section 8-1 of the ITAA 1997 in relation to the acquisition of income units in a hybrid trust in the event of an estimated negative annual return?

   No. You can only claim a deduction equivalent to the amount of assessable income distributions received.

Summary

The comments made by what can only described as uninformed seminar presenters that few accountants are familiar with hybrid trusts is incorrect. They simply understand that they offer doubtful use when considered as a structure to hold investment properties.

Claims that 'The most flexible and efficient way of holding property when negative gearing is through a hybrid discretionary trust' (from www.investorone.com.au) can only lead to problems for property investors who follow this ill-informed advice.

I agree with Nick Renton, author of *Family Trusts*, who says on his website:

> I suspect that the reason that not many accountants or lawyers are familiar with these structures is that the alleged advantages of hybrid trusts over discretionary trusts simply do not exist.
>
> I gather from the various questions to me that some unlicensed persons mention them periodically in lectures as part of a sales spiel.
>
> I have not found anything in the legislation to support the hybrid trust theory. Even if there is some unintended loophole then taxpayers using it would probably expose themselves to penalties under the general anti-avoidance provisions of the tax legislation (Part IVA), so investors contemplating using these devices should be very careful.

Chapter 20

Record keeping

Obligation to keep records

Tax law requires you to maintain records that explain your rental property transactions. They must be kept:

- in writing in the English language or, alternatively, in a form where they are accessible (for example, on computer) and can be converted into written English

- in such a way that your assessable income and allowable deductions can readily be ascertained

- for five years after the issuing of an invoice or completion of the transaction.

These records should include documents that relate to your rental income and expenditure, and acquisition and/or disposal of your rental property.

Although not required to be lodged with your income tax return, the records must be produced if requested.

If you fail to comply with the retention requirements you run the risk of a maximum penalty of $3000.

Agent's rental statements

If you use a real estate agent to manage the property you must retain the monthly statements he or she sends you. I suggest that you prepare a summary spreadsheet (such as the example in appendix C) and give this, together with the statements, to your accountant when you make your annual tax visit.

Separate bank account

I strongly advise that a separate bank account be opened and used solely for rental purposes. This way your rental transactions will be kept separate from your private affairs. The rent received should be banked intact into this account so as to maintain a clear income trail. This can then be reconciled against your rental statements or rent receipt book to ensure that all monies have been accounted for.

All rental expenses should be paid by cheque from this account. The danger of paying in cash is that if you don't record the expenditure it could be overlooked at tax time. This could result in the payment of more tax than you actually owe or the receipt of a smaller return than you are entitled to.

Bank statements

Keep your bank statements in a separate file for each year. Cross-reference the entries to your invoices and receipts.

Number the invoices and record this number next to the entry on the bank statement. File the invoices in numerical order in a separate file. Use the receipt number for the cross-referencing of the income or, if you are using an agent, the month of the agent's rental statement.

Receipts

If you manage the property yourself you should use a pre-numbered receipt book and issue a receipt for the rental received.

Invoices

Invoices for advertising, repairs, cleaning, pest control, rates notices, body corporate fee notifications, land tax bills and power accounts relating to the rental property should be retained, along with any other documentation relating to rental property expenditure. The invoice should show:

- the date of the invoice
- the name of the supplier
- the date the expense was incurred
- the amount of the expense
- the nature of the goods or service.

Motor running

Keep a log book to record the date and kilometres travelled to collect rent, purchase items needed for repairs, inspect the property, visit your accountant and attend to other rental matters. The log book should record the purpose of the trip.

Telephone calls and postage

Each time you use the telephone for rental business, record the date of your call in a notebook. Document the date and amount of stamps purchased when posting items relating to the property.

Insurance policies

Keep the insurance policies relating to the property in a safe place.

Purchase documentation

It is essential that you keep the contract, loan agreement and documentation, and solicitor's settlement statement, along with any other records relating to the purchase of the property. These must be retained for a period of five years after disposal of the property.

Asset valuation

If you use a quantity surveyor to place values on the construction cost and depreciable items, the valuation must be kept for five years after disposal of the property. The account for preparation of the report must be maintained for five years after incurring the cost.

Disposal documentation

If you sell your rental property you must keep the sale contract, solicitor's settlement statement, agent's commission statement and other documentation relating to the sale for five years after the sale.

Reduce your fees

Accountants charge on an hourly basis, and their time is not cheap. Sometimes, they have a fixed fee for certain work. For example, they may charge $200 for an individual income tax return with one rental property. (This is an example only. Rates vary greatly between city and suburban tax agents, and not necessarily in relation to the quality of the job done.) If you hand over cheque butts, bank statements, invoices and rental statements, that fee might rise to $400 because of the extra time involved.

It is in your interest to present the information for preparation of your rental income and expenditure statement as well organised as possible. If you don't, you can expect to be charged for it. If you can't be bothered doing this, don't complain about the extra cost—you will have contributed to it.

Why pay someone to do work you can do yourself? You can categorise and list expenditure, summarise loan statements, prepare rental summaries, note the cost and date of asset acquisitions, and obtain the asset values and cost of construction before going to the accountant. I can assure you he or she will thank you for it.

Pay the accountant for his or her expertise and knowledge in relation to maximising the claims you are entitled to. Rest assured—he or she would rather spend his or her time doing this than collating source records.

Choosing your accountant

As in all professions, there are varying levels of expertise among accountants. However, if your accountant is a member of one of the professional bodies you can be sure that he or she is technically competent. None have magic rabbits to pull out of hats. It is pointless to go from one to another, year to year, looking for the tax agent who can get you a refund when there isn't one there.

Ensure your accountant is also a registered tax agent. If he or she is not, he or she is not permitted to charge a fee for preparation of a tax return.

Members of both the Institute of Chartered Accountants in Australia and the Australian Society of CPAs are required to maintain an appropriate level of continuing professional education each year, thereby ensuring their knowledge base is maintained.

Should you prepare your return yourself?

Our taxation laws are complex and subject to change. The self-assessment system assumes that you have a knowledge of these laws. It is difficult enough for a tax professional to keep abreast of the changes, let alone a layperson. For this reason, if you have rental properties, the costs you will incur through using an accountant will be far less than the costs you may incur on audit if you get it wrong. That doesn't mean that the accountant will not make mistakes, but the chances of error are far less than if you do it yourself. And the chances are that additional legitimate deductions may be found that you had not previously been claiming.

Rental property documentation checklist

Ensure you keep the following documents on file:

☑ settlement statement

☑ purchase and sale contracts

- ☑ title deed
- ☑ loan documentation
- ☑ real estate agency agreements
- ☑ lease
- ☑ bond details
- ☑ quantity surveyor's depreciation report
- ☑ real estate agent statements
- ☑ bank statements
- ☑ loan statements
- ☑ car running diary or log book (for rental usage)
- ☑ invoices and rates notices
- ☑ previous year's tax return.

Chapter 21

Preparing your tax return

The information presented below is based on the 2007 income tax forms. It is presented to help those of you who wish to prepare your own returns without the aid of an accountant or tax agent, or who wish to understand the return that has been prepared for you.

Individuals

1   Rental income and expenditure is declared at item 20 of the tax return for individuals.

2   The rent you received from your tenants should be shown at label P, Gross rent. If you have a commercial rental and GST has been collected, you show the rent excluding GST.

3   Rental from foreign sources is declared at item 19, not here.

4   Interest incurred is claimed under label Q, Interest deductions.

5   Capital works deductions (construction cost allowances) are inserted as label F, Capital works deductions.

6   All other deductions are totalled and included at label U, Other rental deductions. If you have a commercial property and GST has been paid, you should show the GST-excluded amount here. If you are not registered for GST or the property is residential, you claim the full amount incurred. This is because residential properties are input taxed and you are not able to recover GST paid in respect of them on your business activity statement (if you are required to lodge one).

7   The summation of label P less labels Q, F and U is inserted as item 20. If a loss is incurred, you print L in the box to the right of the amount.

Partnerships

1   Rental income and expenditure is declared at item 9 of the partnership income tax return.

2   The rent you received from your tenants should be shown at label F, Gross rent. If you have a commercial rental and GST has been collected, you show the rent excluding GST.

3   Interest incurred is claimed under label G, Interest deductions.

4   Capital works deductions (construction cost allowances) are inserted as label X, Capital works deductions.

5   All other deductions are totalled and included at label H, Other rental deductions. If you have a commercial

property and GST has been paid, you should show the GST-excluded amount here. If you are not registered for GST or the property is residential, you claim the full amount incurred. (For further details, see point 6 under 'Individuals'.)

6   The summation of label P less labels Q, F and U inserted as item 9. If a loss is incurred, you print L in the box to the right of the amount.

Companies

1   Rental income and expenditure is declared at item 6, Calculation of total profit or loss.

2   The rent you received from your tenants should be shown at label G, Gross rent and other leasing and hiring income. If your company has a commercial rental and GST has been collected, you show the rent excluding GST.

3   Interest incurred is claimed under label V, Interest expenses within Australia.

4   Depreciation is claimed at label X, Depreciation expenses.

5   Repairs are claimed at label Z, Repairs and maintenance.

6   All other deductions are totalled and included at label S, All other expenses. If your company has a commercial property and GST has been paid, you should show the GST-excluded amount here. If you are not registered for GST or the property is residential, you claim the full amount incurred. (For further details, see point 6 under 'Individuals'.)

7   Item H, Rent expenses, refers to the expenditure a company incurs as a tenant, not the expenses claimed as a landlord.

Trusts

1   Rental income and expenditure is declared at item 9 of the trust income tax return.

2   The rent you received from your tenants should be shown at label F, Gross rent. If you have a commercial rental and GST has been collected, you show the rent excluding GST.

3   Interest incurred is claimed under label G, Interest deductions.

4   Capital works deductions (construction cost allowances) are inserted as label X, Capital works deductions.

5   All other deductions are totalled and included at label H, Other rental deductions. If the trust has a commercial property and GST has been paid, you should show the GST-excluded amount here. If it is not registered for GST, or the property is residential you claim the full amount incurred. (For further details, see point 6 under 'Individuals'.)

6   The summation of label P less labels Q, F and U is inserted as item 9. If a loss is incurred, you print L in the box to the right of the amount.

Superannuation funds

1   Rental income and expenditure is declared at item 9a.

2   The rent you received by the superannuation fund from its tenants is declared under label B, Gross rent and other leasing and hiring income.

3   Rental property deductions are claimed under item 9b.

4   Construction cost allowances, if applicable, are inserted as label X, Capital works deductions.

5   Decline in value is claimed at label W, deduction for decline in value of depreciating assets.

6   All other rental deductions are included under label L, Investment expenses.

Rental statements

For 2005, tax agents lodging partnership or trust tax return through ELS were required to complete a 'Partnerships and trusts rental property schedule' if rent was received. This was not required if a paper version of the return was lodged. As a matter of prudence, it is wise to complete one for your own records. An example is shown in figure 21.1.

Figure 21.1: sample rental property schedule

```
                          Draft                    TFN:        Page 1 of 1
        2005 Rental Property Statement

    Address of Rental Property



    Date property first earned rental income
    Number of weeks property was rented this year

    Number of weeks property was available for rent this year
    What is the entity's % ownership of the property?
    Date property was purchased
    Purchase price of property

    Date property was sold (if property disposed of during year)
    Sale price of property
    Capital gain/loss on sale of this property                          /
    Value of capital allowances (depreciation on plant) recouped on the sale
    Value of capital works deductions (special building write-off) recouped

    Has the loan for the property been renegotiated this year?

    Ownership                                       % owned
        Draft                          RENT0001     100.00
    Income                                          Return
        Gross rental income
        Other rental related income

        Gross Rent
```

(cont'd overleaf)

Figure 21.1 *(cont'd)*: sample rental property schedule

Expenses		Total	Prv %	Return
D	Advertising for tenants			0
E	Body corporate fees			0
F	Borrowing expenses			0
G	Cleaning			0
H	Council Rates			0
I	Capital allowances (depreciation)			0
J	Gardening/lawn mowing			0
K	Insurance			0
L	Interest on loans			0
M	Land Tax			0
N	Legal fees			0
O	Pest control			0
P	Property agent fees/commission			0
Q	Repairs and maintenance			0
R	Capital works-special build w/off			0
S	Stationery, telephone and postage			0
T	Travel expenses			0
U	Water charges			0
V	Sundry rental expenses			0
Total expenses		0		0
Net Rent		0 /		0 /

Chapter 22

Technical matters

Up to now I have deliberately refrained, where possible, from referring to specific sections of Australia's tax legislation. I am firmly of the opinion that other than for tax professionals, it is more important to know that something does or does not have a tax effect rather than the section of the legislation, or the particular case that explains the effect. However, some readers may require a more specific treatise. For that I refer them to CCH Australia's or LexisNexis/Butterworths' publications, and the Tax Acts. Others may find the selection of technical matters presented below to be adequate information.

Our income tax laws are constantly under review. What is law today may well not be tomorrow. The Tax Law Improvement Project had the task of rewriting the income tax law to make it easier to understand. As a result, our tax legislation, at the time of writing, is largely embodied in two principal Acts. These are the *Income Tax Assessment Act 1936* as amended and the *Income Tax Assessment Act 1997*.

The 1997 Act contained the first instalments of the rewritten provisions. Future amendments will be inserted as additional provisions into this Act. The 1997 Act renumbers sections of the old Act as well as rewriting them. For this reason, references are limited to the new Act.

Income: section 6-5

Income from rental properties is assessable under section 6-5 of the Act.

Income according to ordinary concepts (ordinary income)

6-5(1) Your assessable income includes income according to ordinary concepts, which is called ordinary income.

6-5(2) If you are an Australian resident, your assessable income includes the ordinary income you derived directly or indirectly from all sources, whether in or out of Australia, during the income year.

6-5(3) If you are not an Australian resident, your assessable income includes:

a   the ordinary income you derived directly or indirectly from all Australian sources during the income year; and

b   other ordinary income that a provision includes in your assessable income for the income year on some basis other than having an Australian source.

6-5(4) In working out whether you have derived an amount of ordinary income, and (if so) when you derived it, you are taken to have received the amount as soon as it is applied or dealt with in any way on your behalf or as you direct.

Deductions: section 8-1

The majority of deductible items fall under section 8-1 of the 1997 Act—'General deductions':

8-1(1) You can deduct from your assessable income any loss or outgoing to the extent that:

a   it is incurred in gaining or producing your assessable income; or

b   it is necessarily incurred in carrying on a business for the purpose of gaining or producing your assessable income.

8-1(2) However, you cannot deduct a loss or outgoing under this section to the extent that:

a   it is a loss or outgoing of capital, or of a capital nature; or

b   it is a loss or outgoing of a private or domestic nature; or

c   it is incurred in relation to gaining or producing your exempt income; or

d   a provision of this Act prevents you from deducting it.

For a summary list of provisions about deductions, see section 12-5.

8-1(3) A loss or outgoing that you can deduct under this section is called a general deduction.

Expenses such as advertising, bank charges and agent's commissions fall under these provisions.

Other claims are specifically covered by other parts of the Acts.

Borrowing costs: section 25-25

25-25(1) You can deduct expenditure you incur for borrowing money, to the extent that you use the money for the purpose of producing assessable income. In most cases the deduction is spread over the period of the loan.

For cases where the deduction is not spread, see subsection (6).

Note: Your deductions under this section may be reduced if any of your commercial debts have been forgiven in the income year: see subdivision 245-E of schedule 2C to the *Income Tax Assessment Act 1936*.

Income year when money used solely for the purpose of producing assessable income

25-25(2) You can deduct for an income year the maximum amount worked out under subsection (4) if you use the borrowed money during that income year solely for the purpose of producing assessable income.

Example

In 1997–98 you borrow $100 000 and incur expenditure of $1500 for the borrowing. You use the money to buy a house. Throughout 1998–99 you rent the house to a tenant. You can deduct for the expenditure for 1998–99 the maximum amount subsection (4).

Income year when borrowed money used partly for that purpose

25-25(3) If you use the money only partly for that purpose during that income year, you can deduct the proportion of that maximum amount that is appropriate having regard to the extent that you used the borrowed money for that purpose.

Note: You cannot deduct anything for that income year if you do not use the money for that purpose at all during that income year.

Maximum deduction for an income year

25-25(4) You work out as follows the maximum amount that you can deduct for the expenditure for an income year:

Method statement

Step 1   Work out the remaining expenditure as follows below.

- For the income year in which the period of the loan begins, it is the amount of the expenditure.

- For a later income year, it is the amount of the expenditure reduced by the maximum amount that you can deduct for the expenditure for each earlier income year.

Step 2   Work out the remaining loan period as follows overleaf.

- For the income year in which the period of the loan begins, it is the period of the loan (as determined at the end of the income year).

- For a later income year, it is the period from the start of the income year until the end of the period of the loan (as determined at the end of the income year).

Step 3   Divide the remaining expenditure by the number of days in the remaining loan period.

Step 4   Multiply the result from step 3 by the number of days in the remaining loan period that are in the income year.

Example

To continue the example in subsection (2): suppose the original period of the loan is four years starting on 1 September 1997. What is the maximum amount you can deduct for the expenditure for 1997–98?

Applying the method statement

After step 1:   the remaining expenditure is $1500 (the amount of the expenditure).

After step 2:   the remaining loan period is 4 years from 1 September 1997 (1461 days).

After step 3:   the result is $1500 divided by 1461 = $1.03.

After step 4:   the result is $1.03 multiplied by 302 days = $310.06.

Suppose you repay the loan early, on 31 December 1998. What is the maximum amount you can deduct for the expenditure for 1998–99?

Applying the method statement

After step 1:   the remaining expenditure is $1500 (the amount of the expenditure) reduced by $310.06 (the maximum amount you can deduct for 1997–98) = $1189.94.

After step 2:   the remaining loan period is the period from 1 July 1998 to 31 December 1998 (183 days).

After step 3:   the result is $1189.94 divided by 183 days = $6.50.

After step 4:   the result is $6.50 multiplied by 183 days = $1189.94.

Meaning of period of the loan

25-25(5) The period of the loan is the shortest of these periods:

a   the period of the loan as specified in the original loan contract;

b   the period starting on the first day on which the money was borrowed and ending on the day the loan is repaid;

c   five years starting on the first day on which the money was borrowed.

When deduction is not spread

25-25(6) If the total of the following is $100 or less:

a   each amount of expenditure you incur in an income year for borrowing money you use during that income year solely for the purpose of producing assessable income;

b   for each amount of expenditure you incur in that income year for borrowing money you use during that income year only partly for that purpose—the proportion of that amount that is appropriate having regard to the extent that you use the money during that income year for that purpose;

you can deduct for the income year:

c   each amount covered by paragraph (a); and

d   each proportion covered by paragraph (b).

Decline in value: section 42-15

42-15 You deduct an amount for depreciation of a unit of plant for an income year if, in that year:

a   you are its owner or quasi-owner; and

b   you use it, or have it installed ready for use, for the purpose of producing assessable income.

Note: If there is a quasi-owner, the owner cannot deduct: see section 42-320.

Amount you deduct: section 42-20

42-20(1) The amount you deduct is worked out under subdivision 42-E. However, for plant in a pool, you work out the amount under subdivision 42-L.

42-20(2) You cannot deduct more than the undeducted cost of the plant.

Calculation: section 42-25

42-25(1) The calculation of your deduction is based on the cost of the plant to you.

42-25(2) The rate you use to calculate your deduction is set out in subdivision 42-D. Generally, the rate is based on the effective life of the plant.

42-25(3) You have a choice of 2 calculation methods: the diminishing value method and the prime cost method. You make the choice for the income year in which a depreciation deduction is first allowable to you for the plant.

Note: The diminishing value method calculates your deduction each year as a percentage of the balance you have left to deduct.

The prime cost method calculates your deduction each year as a percentage of your cost.

Balancing adjustments: section 42-30

42-30(1) You must make a balancing adjustment calculation for plant if:

a   you have deducted or can deduct an amount for depreciation of it or, if Common Rule 1 (roll-over relief for related entities) applied to your acquisition of it, the transferor or an earlier successive transferor deducted or can deduct an amount for depreciation of it; and

b   a balancing adjustment event occurs.

Note 1: However, no balancing adjustment calculation is required if Common Rule 1 applies to the balancing adjustment event.

Note 2: A balancing adjustment calculation may include an amount in your assessable income or allow you to deduct an amount. If you are required to include an amount in your assessable income, balancing adjustment relief may be available: see sections 42-285, 42-290 and 42-295.

42-30(2) Balancing adjustments are calculated under:

a   subdivision 42-F; or

b   subdivision 42-G for some cars; or

c   section 42-390 for plant in a pool.

42-30(3) A balancing adjustment event occurs as shown in table 22.1.

Table 22.1: balancing adjustment event

If you are:		When:
The owner of plant	a	you dispose of it and do not become its quasi-owner; or
	b	it is lost or destroyed; or
	c	subsection 42-330(2) applies
The quasi-owner of plant	a	you cease to be the quasi-owner of it and do not become its owner
	b	it is lost or destroyed; or
	c	subsection 42-330(2) applies

Note: Section 42-330 deals with partial change of ownership.

Adjustment: previously depreciated plant: section 42-90

42-90(1) The Commissioner may limit the cost to you of plant for which an amount has been deducted or can be deducted for depreciation by any earlier owner or quasi-owner.

42-90(2) The cost of the plant may be limited to the sum of:

a   its written-down value, immediately before the balancing adjustment event occurred, in the hands of the last entity who had deducted or can deduct an amount for depreciation of it; and

b   any balancing adjustment included in that entity's assessable income for the plant under Subdivision 42-F or 42-G; and

c   any balancing adjustment that would have been included in that entity's assessable income for the plant if balancing adjustment relief under Section 42-285 (same year relief) or 42-290 (later year relief) had not applied.

42-90(3) If the last entity had the plant in a pool for the income year in which the balancing adjustment event occurred, its cost may be limited to the sum of:

a   any balancing adjustment included in that entity's assessable income for the plant under section 42-390; and

b   any balancing adjustment that would have been included in that entity's assessable income for the plant if balancing adjustment relief under section 42-285 or 42-290 had not applied.

42-90(4) The matters to be taken into account by the Commissioner in deciding whether to limit the cost of plant include:

a   whether you acquired the plant from an associate; and

b   the market value of the plant; and

c   how the purchase price of the plant was calculated; and

d   how the acquisition was financed; and

e   whether the plant is for use by the entity from whom you acquired it or by an associate of the entity.

Discharge of mortgage: section 25-30

Mortgage for borrowed money

25-30(1) You can deduct expenditure you incur to discharge a mortgage that you gave as security for the repayment of money that you borrowed if you used the money solely for the purpose of producing assessable income.

Mortgage for property bought

25-30(2) You can deduct expenditure you incur to discharge a mortgage that you gave as security for the payment of the whole or part of the purchase price of property that you bought if you used the property solely for the purpose of producing assessable income.

Money or property used partly for that purpose

25-30(3) If you used the money you borrowed, or the property you bought, only partly for the purpose of producing assessable income, you can deduct the expenditure to the extent that you used the money or property for that purpose.

No deduction for payments of principal or interest

25-30(4) You cannot deduct payments of principal or interest under this section.

Lease document expenses

25-20(1) You can deduct expenditure you incur for preparing, registering or stamping:

a   a lease of property; or

b   an assignment or surrender of a lease of property;

if you have used or will use the property solely for the purpose of producing assessable income.

Property used partly for that purpose

25-20(2) If you have used, or will use, the leased property only partly for that purpose, you can deduct the expenditure to the extent that you have used, or will use, the leased property for that purpose.

Repairs and maintenance: section 25-20

25-10(1) You can deduct expenditure you incur for repairs to premises (or part of premises), plant, machinery, tools or articles that you held or used solely for the purpose of producing assessable income.

Property held or used partly for that purpose

25-10(2) If you held or used the property only partly for that purpose, you can deduct so much of the expenditure as is reasonable in the circumstances.

No deduction for capital expenditure

25-10(3) You cannot deduct capital expenditure under this section.

Cases

Our legal system is based on the English common law system. This means that it is based on legislation and the interpretation of that legislation. Hence there are many cases that determine what the statutes mean. Some cases that relate to rental income and expenditure are noted below.

Apportionment

Case R118, 84 ATC 773

Where rent is received from a short-term letting, the expenses are apportioned on a time basis in accordance with the period the property is let. The taxpayer owned a holiday home which, although available for rent at any time, was let for only five weeks in a year. The court determined rental income was a relatively minor objective and reduced the claims to 20 per cent.

Kowal; FC of T v 84 ATC 4001

Where a rental has both business and private elements, there is a need to apportion expenses.

Depreciation

Case 11/97

Kitchen cupboards were found to be part of the infrastructure of a unit, not plant, and were therefore not depreciable.

Family home

Janmor Nominees Pty Ltd; FC of T v 87 ATC 4813

The earning of assessable income and claiming of allowable deductions for a family home owned by a family trust was acceptable as it involved a commercial transaction.

Interest

Fletcher v FCT [1990] 92 ATC 4611

Interest on a transaction entered into predominantly to create a tax deduction with no view to returning a profit was found to be non-deductible.

Case 63/96, 96 ATC 578

A refinancing of a joint loan used to finance a rental property into a loan to the spouse was ineffective.

Steele v FC of T ATC 4239

On appeal to the High Court it was found that interest paid regarding a development of a motel-style complex could be claimed as a deduction during the construction phase. This is a development since previous printings of this book where the situation was that the interest was capital because it was in relation to the creation of a capital asset that was not earning any income.

Rent paid in advance

Case B51, 70 ATC 253

Rent was received covering the term of the lease (which was over several years). No part of the rent was refundable. It was held that the rent was assessable when received.

Case B47, 70 ATC 236

Rent was received in advance, with a weekly rental specified, but a right of proportionate refund upon termination existed. It was found that only the rent relating to the expired part of the lease was assessable when received.

Repairs

Lurcott v Wakeley and Wheeler (1911) 1 KB 905

Established that 'the question of repair is in every case one of degree and the test is whether the act to be done is one which in substance is the renewal or replacement of defective parts, or the renewal or replacement of substantially the whole'.

Case S94, 85 ATC 681

Expenses incurred in painting a property, known to need repainting at the time of purchase, were not allowable.

Case W7, 89 ATC 161

Renovations required at the time of purchase to bring the property into a desirable condition were found to be expenses of acquisition and not deductible.

[1951] 2 T.B.R.D., Case B38

Expenditure on alterations to bring a rented property up to council by-laws standard were an outgoing of capital and not deductible.

Case V167, 88 ATC 1107

Replacement of kitchen cupboards and fittings was held to be a restructuring and not a repair. The expenses were not deductible.

Case J24, 77 ATC 222

The replacement of a dilapidated wooden fence with a block and brick wall was an improvement and not a repair.

Token rent

Groser, FC of T v 82 ATC 4478

Where a rental is only a token amount the Tax Office may treat the rent as a domestic arrangement with no tax effect. Note the rental involved in this case was $2 per week.

Travel

Case C71, 71 ATC 315

Travel costs to inspect properties with the view to purchase for rental were not allowable.

Rulings

From time to time the Tax Office issues rulings which set out its interpretation of the legislation. These are not law but are binding and can be relied upon by a taxpayer. Rulings are sometimes withdrawn—for example, on 2 July 1997 the following rulings with relevance to rental properties were withdrawn:

- IT 166: interest on money borrowed to acquire an income-producing asset

- 2374 Income Tax: loss from rental property before being leased
- 2461 Income Tax: deductibility of outgoings incurred before income derived from undeveloped land.

A sample listing of rulings and determinations which are current at the time of writing and relevant to rental properties follows.

Borrowing costs

TD 93/48 income tax: is a deduction for borrowing costs allowable under section 67 of the *Income Tax Assessment Act 1936* when a loan does not proceed.

Co-ownership

TR 93/32 income tax: rental property—division of net income or loss between co-owners.

Depreciation

IT 7 rates of depreciation: curtains and drapes.

IT 242 depreciation: on hot water installations, stoves, etc. in income-producing properties.

IT 2685 income tax: depreciation.

TR 2001/18C9 income tax: effective life of depreciating asset.

TR 2004/16 income tax: plant in residential properties.

Interest

TR 93/7 income tax: whether penalty interest payments are deductible.

TR 93/21 income tax: timing of deductions for discounts on commercial bills with a term of less than 12 months.

TR 95/25 income tax: deductions for interest under subsection 51(1) of the *Income Tax Assessment Act 1936* following *FC of T v Roberts*; *FC of T v Smith.*

TR 98/22 income tax: the taxation consequences for taxpayers entering into certain linked or split loan facilities.

TR 2000/17 income tax: deductions for interest following the Steele and Brown decision.

TR 2000/2 income tax: deductibility of interest on moneys drawn down under line of credit facilities and redraw.

TR 2004/04 interest: when no assessable income received.

IT 2661 income tax: apportionment of interest where money is borrowed to fund the purchase of an asset part of which is used for a business purpose and part for a non-business purpose.

Non–arms-length rentals

IT 2167 income tax: rental properties—non-economic rental, holiday home, share of residence and family trust cases.

Outgoings

TR 95/33 income tax: subsection 51(1)—relevance of subjective purpose, motive or intention in determining the deductibility of losses and outgoings.

Repairs and improvements

Copies of these rulings may be obtained from the Tax Office. The following legislation is part of the *A New Tax System (Goods and Services Tax) Act 1999.*

Residential rent: subdivision 40-B, section 40-35

40-35 (1) A supply of premises that is by way of lease, hire or licence (including a renewal or extension of a lease, hire or licence) is input taxed if:

a   the supply is of residential premises (other than commercial residential premises); or

b   the supply is of commercial accommodation and division 87 (which is about long-term accommodation in commercial premises) would apply to the supply but for a choice made by the supplier under section 87-25.

40-35 (2) However:

a   the supply is input taxed only to the extent that the premises are to be used predominantly for residential accommodation; and

b   the supply is not input taxed under this section if the lease, hire or licence, or the renewal or extension of a lease, hire or licence, is a long-term lease.

Residential premises: subdivision 40-C

Sales of residential premises

40-65 (1) A sale of real property is input taxed, but only to the extent that the property is residential premises to be used predominantly for residential accommodation.

40-65 (2) However, the sale is not input taxed to the extent that the residential premises are commercial residential premises or new residential premises.

Supplies of residential premises by way of long-term lease

40-70 (1) A supply is input taxed if:

a   the supply is of real property but only to the extent that the property is residential premises to be used predominantly for residential accommodation; and

b   the supply is by way of long-term lease.

40-70 (2) However, the supply is not input taxed to the extent that the residential premises are commercial residential premises or new residential premises.

Chapter 23

Land tax

Land tax is assessed annually by all states, the ACT but not the Northern Territory. It is based on the unimproved value of land after deducting applicable exemptions. Land tax paid on an income-producing property is an allowable deduction. The rates are shown in table 23.1.

Table 23.1: land tax rates

Land value	Rate
Australian Capital Territory	
Residential properties	
Up to $75 000	0.60%
$75 001 to $150 000	0.89%
$150 001 to $275 000	1.15%
$275 001 and over	1.4%

Commercial properties

Up to $150000	0.89%
$150001 to $275000	1.25%
$275001 and over	1.59%

New South Wales

Below $352000	Nil
$352 001 and over	$100 plus 1.7% of the value exceeding $352000

Queensland

Individuals

Up to $449999	Nil
$450000 to $749999	$400 plus 0.7% of the excess over $500000
$750000 to $1249999	$2500 plus 1.45% of the excess over $750000
$1250000 to $1999999	$9750 plus 1.5% of the excess over $1250000
$2000000 to $2999999	$21000 plus 1.65% of the excess over $2000000
$3000000 and over	Flat rate of 1.25%

Companies, absentees and trustees

Up to $349999	Nil
$350000 to $749999	$2250 plus 1.5% of the excess over $300000
$750000 to $1249999	$8250 plus 1.65% of the excess over $750000
$1250000 to $1999999	$16500 plus 1.8% of the excess over $1250000
$2000000 and over	Flat rate of 1.25%

Land tax

South Australia	
Up to $110 000	Nil
$110 001 to $350 000	3% of the excess over $110 000
$350 001 to $550 000	$720 plus 0.7% of the excess over $350 000
$550 001 to $750 000	$2120 plus 1.65% of the excess over $550 000
$750 001 to $1 000 000	$5240 plus 2.4% of the excess over $750 000
$1 000 000 and over	$11 420 plus 3.7% of the excess over $1 000 000

Tasmania	
Up to $25 000	Nil
$25 000 to $349 999	$500 plus 0.55% of the excess over $25 000
$350 000 to $749 999	$1837.50 plus 2% of the excess over $350 000
$750 000 and over	$9837.50 plus 2% of the excess over $750 000

Victoria	
Up to $199 000	Nil
$200 000 to $539 999	$200 plus 0.2% of the excess over $200 000
$540 000 to $899 999	$880 plus 0.5% of the excess over $540 000
$900 000 to $1 189 999	$2680 plus 0.8% of the excess over $900 000
$1 190 000 to $1 619 999	$5000 plus 1.2% of the excess over $1 190 000
$1 650 000 to $2 699 999	$10 160 plus 1.8% of the excess over $1 620 000
$2 700 000 and over	$18 500 plus 3% of the excess over $2 700 000

Western Australia	
Up to $250 000	Nil
$250 000 to $875 000	0.15% of the excess over $250 000
$875 000 to $2 000 000	$937.50 plus 0.75% of the excess over $875 000
$2 000 000 to $5 000 000	$9375 plus 1.3% of the excess over $2 000 000
$5 000 000 to $10 000 000	$48 375 plus 1.55% of the excess over $5 000 000
$10 000 000 and over	$125 875 plus 2.3% of the excess over $10 000 000

Exemptions and deductions

Exemptions and deductions differ from state to state. At the time of writing, they include, but are not restricted to, the following.

Australian Capital Territory

- principal place of residence

- primary production land

- rented but the owner is temporarily absent (for a maximum of 12 months) for a compelling compassionate reason.

New South Wales

- principal place of residence not owned by a company or trustee

- home units under strata title occupied by the owner or one or more of the joint owners as his or her principal residence

- primary production land (in most circumstances).

Queensland

- principal place of residence

- primary production land with provisos.

South Australia

- principal place of residence

- primary production land with provisos.

Tasmania

- principal residence

- rural land

- landowners receiving total and permanent disabled pensions, and pensioners holding a current pensioner concession card (with conditions).

Victoria

- principal residence

- primary production land.

Western Australia

- principal place of residence where all the owners reside and which is used solely or principally as a residence

- primary production land.

The above lists of exemptions and deductions are not exhaustive. Various other exemptions apply from state to state.

Conclusion

This book was written in an attempt to help non-taxation professionals who own, or are considering to own, a rental property understand their obligations under the Australian income tax laws. It is not a guide as to how to purchase rental properties, or a discussion of the merits or otherwise of rental property investment. Many other books exist on those subjects. For those wishing to read such a title, I strongly recommend *Realistic Real Estate Investing* by Austin Donnelly (published by Wrightbooks).

Apart from where necessary, and the chapter on technical matters, I attempted to refrain as much as possible from quoting section numbers and case details from tax law. If, by reading this book, you have gained a clearer understanding of the taxation laws as they relate to rental properties, I have succeeded in my aim. If not, then hopefully the book has raised some questions that will prompt you to ask why, for taxation reasons, you should not accept some of the many real estate investment myths.

In discussing matters such as negative gearing, types of loans and ownership structures, I have attempted to provide information that will enable you to come to your own conclusions. We all have different circumstances, and those circumstances change. Each proposal should be viewed with that in mind.

Some will argue that my long-term analysis in chapter 17 does not consider the time value of money. That may be, but my purpose was to emphasise, in simple terms, that careful thought should be given to the long-term consequences of purchasing a rental property in the name of the family breadwinner.

While conducting the research for this book, my perceptions as to the income levels of rental property investors changed. They did not reflect the profile in my practice. I was amazed at the number of investors on lower incomes who quoted negative gearing as a consideration in their rental property purchase. This confirmed my comment in the preface that the majority of investors do not understand the tax implications of their property investment.

The names in the examples in the book have been changed so as to protect the identity of my clients. Without my clients I would not have an accountancy practice, and I would not have gained the experience to enable me to write this book. I thank every one of them.

Appendix A

Deduction checklist

The checklist that follows may assist you in ensuring you claim the deductions you are entitled to in respect of your rental property. These deductions were discussed in chapter 2.

Deductible

☑ advertising

☑ agents' fees and commission for collecting rent and management of the rental property

☑ bank charges for deposits of rent and payment of expenses

☑ body corporate fees (other than a special levy for capital work)

☑ borrowing costs to finance the property

☑ building cost amortised after 17 July 1985, and structural improvements amortised after 26 February 1992

☑ cleaning

☑ computer costs

☑ decline in value (depreciation)

☑ gardening and grounds maintenance

- ☑ in-house movie and video costs
- ☑ insurance (building, fire, burglary, public liability, rent protection)
- ☑ interest on late payment of rates
- ☑ interest on loans to finance the property
- ☑ land tax
- ☑ lease costs
- ☑ lease incentive payments
- ☑ legal costs to recover rent owing or breach of agreements
- ☑ letting fees
- ☑ linen hire
- ☑ management fees
- ☑ mortgage insurance
- ☑ mortgage release fees
- ☑ motor running
- ☑ PABX fees
- ☑ penalty interest
- ☑ pest control
- ☑ security patrol fees
- ☑ stationery, postage and printing
- ☑ rates
- ☑ rates, water and land tax adjustments upon purchase
- ☑ refinancing costs
- ☑ rental property depreciation reports (quantity surveyor's fees)

☑ repairs and maintenance

☑ safe deposit boxes

☑ secretarial and bookkeeping expenses

☑ tax agent and accountant's fees

☑ telephone calls regarding management of the property

☑ travel relating to rent collection, inspection of property or attending to repairs

Non-deductible

☒ body corporate fees—special contributions for capital works (however, can claim structural)

☒ cost of relocating depreciable assets from one property to another

☒ deposit bond fees

☒ early lease surrender costs

☒ improvements (however, write off when the work is completed)

☒ initial improvements

☒ legal fees on purchasing property, or defending title

☒ life insurance required by lender

☒ property investment seminars

☒ stamp duty on purchase of property

☒ travel relating to the purchase of property, pre-settlement inspections or attending to property improvements

Pro forma agent's statement summary

Agent's statement summary
5 Zeeman Street, Springwood
Year ended 30 June 2008

Month	Rent ($)	Commission ($)	Agent's costs ($)	Letting fees ($)	Lawn-mowing ($)	Carpet ($)	Repairs ($)	Cheque ($)
July	660	49.52	1.70					608.78
August	825	61.88	1.70					761.42
September	330	24.75	1.70					303.55
October	990	74.25	1.70					914.05
November	660	49.52	1.70					608.78
December	825	61.88	1.70				65.00	696.42
January	660	49.52	1.70				41.00	567.78
February	330	24.75	0.85					304.40
March	1085	81.34	0.85	165	175	473	58.60	131.21
April	660	49.52	1.70					608.78
May	660	49.52	1.70					608.78
June	660	49.52	1.70				76.00	532.78
	8345	625.97	18.70	165.00	175.00	473.00	240.60	6646.73

Appendix C

Pro forma rental statement

Statement of rental income and expenditure

5 Zeeman Street, Springwood

Year ended 30 June 2008

Date property first became income-producing: 13 July 2003

Income ($)

Rent received		8 345
Bond recovered		200
		8 545

Expenditure ($)

Administrative charges	19	
Bank charges	32	
Borrowing costs	220	
Depreciation	928	
Construction cost write-off	1 750	
Commission	626	
Insurance	215	
Interest	7 504	
Lawn-mowing	175	
Letting fee	165	
Motor running	212	
Rates	1 177	
Repairs	241	
Telephone	8	
	13 272	13 272
Net loss ($)		**4 727**

Appendix D

Pro forma decline in value schedule

Depreciation schedule
5 Zeeman Street, Springwood
Year ended 30 June 2008

Descrip-tion	Cost ($)	OWDV* ($)	Additions date	Cost ($)	Value ($)	Rate (%)	Type	Deprec. ($)	CWDV** ($)
Carpet	1 500	908			908	25	D	227	
Carpet	473		15/03/97	473	473	25	D	35	
Curtains	140	860			860	30	D	258	
Hot-water system	740	620			620	20	D	124	
Refrig-erator	700	530			530	20	D	106	
Stove	680	420			420	20	D	84	
Washing machine	540		01/12/96	540	540	30	D	94	
	4 773	3 338		1 013	4 351			928	3 423

* Opening written-down value

** Closing written-down value

Appendix E

After-tax cost of interest

The table below shows the after-tax cost of interest at the varying marginal tax rates (including the 1.5 per cent Medicare levy). For example, an interest rate of 7 per cent is equivalent to a rate of 3.75 per cent after tax to a person on the highest marginal rate.

Interest rate %	Marginal tax rates			
	16.5%	31.5%	41.5%	46.5%
6.00	5.01	4.11	3.51	3.21
6.25	5.22	4.35	3.66	3.34
6.50	5.43	4.45	3.80	3.48
6.75	5.64	4.62	3.95	3.61
7.00	5.85	4.80	4.10	3.75
7.25	6.05	4.97	4.24	3.88
7.50	6.26	5.14	4.39	4.01
7.75	6.47	5.31	4.53	4.15
8.00	6.68	5.48	4.68	4.28
8.25	6.89	5.65	4.83	4.41
8.50	7.10	5.82	4.97	4.55
8.75	7.31	5.99	5.12	4.68
9.00	7.52	6.17	5.27	4.82
9.25	7.72	6.34	5.41	4.95
9.50	7.93	6.51	5.56	5.08
9.75	8.14	6.68	5.70	5.22
10.00	8.35	6.85	5.85	5.35

(cont'd overleaf)

Rental Property and Taxation

Interest rate %	Marginal tax rates			
	16.5%	31.5%	41.5%	46.5%
10.25	8.56	7.02	6.00	5.48
10.50	8.77	7.19	6.14	5.62
10.75	8.98	7.36	6.29	5.75
11.00	9.19	7.54	6.44	5.89
11.25	9.39	7.71	6.58	6.02
11.50	9.60	7.88	6.73	6.15
11.75	9.81	8.05	6.87	6.29
12.00	10.02	8.22	7.02	6.42

Index

Index

If you found this book useful …

… then you might like to know about other similar books published by John Wiley & Sons. For more information visit our website <www.johnwiley.com.au/trade>, or if you would like to be sent more details about other books in related areas please photocopy and return the completed coupon below to:

> P/T info
> John Wiley & Sons Australia, Ltd
> 155 Cremorne Street
> Richmond Vic 3121

If you prefer you can reply via email to:
> <aus_pt_info@johnwiley.com.au>.

Please send me information about books on the following areas of interest:

☐   sharemarket (Australian)

☐   sharemarket (global)

☐   property/real estate

☐   taxation and superannuation

☐   general business.

Name:

Address:

Email:

Please note that your details will not be added to any mailing list without your consent.

Printed in Australia
02 Oct 2024
LP035528